T0222520

POLITICS IN SOFTWARE DEVELOPMENT

NAVIGATING STAKEHOLDER POWER AND CONFLICT IN ORGANIZATIONS

Peter Wendorff

Apress®

Politics in Software Development: Navigating Stakeholder Power and Conflict in Organizations

Peter Wendorff
Birmingham, UK

ISBN-13 (pbk): 978-1-4842-7379-1   ISBN-13 (electronic): 978-1-4842-7380-7
https://doi.org/10.1007/978-1-4842-7380-7

Managing Director, Apress Media LLC: Welmoed Spahr
Acquisitions Editor: Shivangi Ramachandran
Development Editor: Matthew Moodie
Coordinating Editor: Mark Powers

Cover designed by eStudioCalamar

Distributed to the book trade worldwide by Apress Media, LLC, 1 New York Plaza, New York, NY 10004, U.S.A. Phone 1-800-SPRINGER, fax (201) 348-4505, e-mail orders-ny@springer-sbm.com, or visit www.springeronline.com. Apress Media, LLC is a California LLC and the sole member (owner) is Springer Science + Business Media Finance Inc (SSBM Finance Inc). SSBM Finance Inc is a **Delaware** corporation.

For information on translations, please e-mail booktranslations@springernature.com; for reprint, paperback, or audio rights, please e-mail bookpermissions@springernature.com.

Apress titles may be purchased in bulk for academic, corporate, or promotional use. eBook versions and licenses are also available for most titles. For more information, reference our Print and eBook Bulk Sales web page at http://www.apress.com/bulk-sales.

Printed on acid-free paper

Contents

About the Author... vii

Introduction ix

Part I: Power and Conflict I

Chapter I: Fundamental Concepts 3

    Stakeholder 3

    Goal 4

    Conflict..5

    Power..6

    Political Behavior 6

    Political Process 7

    Political Tactic..8

    Political Strategy..8

Chapter 2: Perspectives on Power II

    Unitarism II

    Pluralism.. 13

    Bases of Power.. 15

    Dimensions of Power... 17

Chapter 3: Latent Conflict 21

    Causes of Conflict 21

    Stages of Conflict.. 23

    Guarded Communication 24

    Strategic Ambiguity 25

Chapter 4: Open Conflict 29

    Allowing Conflict.. 29

    Behavior Styles.. 30

    Resolution by Hierarchy 32

    Resolution by Politics... 33

Part II: Software Processes 37

Chapter 5: Process Design 39

Process Industry 39

Illustrative Processes 41

    Unified Process (UP) 42

    Extreme Programming (XP) 43

    Scrum 44

Authority Structure 45

Informal Power 47

Organizational Control 49

Chapter 6: Bureaucratic Control 53

Bureaucracy 53

Managers 56

Automation 57

Alternatives 58

Chapter 7: Cultural Control 61

Self-Organizing Teams 61

Organizational Culture 64

Cultural Engineering 67

Leadership 70

Peer Pressure 72

Unobtrusive Control 75

Part III: Political Action 79

Chapter 8: Politics at Work 81

Politics Is Pervasive 81

Political Skill 84

Learning Politics 87

Political Ethics 89

Chapter 9: Political Analysis 95

Analytical Framework 95

Framework Development 98

Related Work 100

Evaluation and Limitations 102

Chapter 10: Political Tactics..105

    Building Power 105

    Limiting Power 109

    Setting Agendas...110

    Framing Issues...113

    Providing Information...115

    Mobilizing Support 118

    Creating Commitment 120

Conclusion 125

References..131

Index...135

About the Author

Peter Wendorff has 25 years of professional experience as an IT consultant focusing on the development of modern information systems with Microsoft technologies. Peter takes great interest in academic research and has presented 24 research papers at conferences. He works as a business consultant and academic adviser through his company Software Research Ltd in the UK. Peter holds master's degrees in software engineering (with distinction, 1999, UK) and business administration (with distinction, 2008, UK), besides corresponding German university degrees.

Introduction

If people say that there are political reasons for a decision in an organization, it usually has a negative connotation. It expresses frustration that the decision-making process does not only depend on rational arguments but also other factors. The interests of influential stakeholders are such factors, and they often dominate decisions in organizations.

Decisions in organizations are a frequent target of political interference, but other aspects of organizational life can become subject to the political behavior of stakeholders too. The term "organizational politics" is used to refer to the political behavior of stakeholders in organizations. Two terms that essentially mean the same are "office" and "workplace" politics.

Stakeholder behavior in organizations is political if it involves the use of power to achieve goals that conflict with the goals of other stakeholders. If stakeholders with conflicting goals engage in political behavior and struggle with one another to achieve their preferred outcomes, they participate in political processes.

Effective participation in political processes requires power. In the case of individuals in organizations, their positions, which give them status and formal authority, are the most visible base of power, but it is by far not the only one. For example, relevant expert knowledge is another valuable base in many political processes. Another one, which is often potent as well as controversial, is suggested by the adage, "[i]t is not what you know but who you know."

Political processes frequently involve stakeholders with very different goals. In such cases, the stakeholders often achieve conflict resolution through an agreement that reconciles the stakeholder goals in a way that is acceptable to all of them. Sometimes the compromise is politically viable but not practicable. It is a serious problem and often leads to software projects which are started but are so under-resourced that they have virtually no chance of success.

The problem has been so prevalent in the software industry that Edward Yourdon (2003) wrote a popular book with the title *Death March* about these projects. In it, Yourdon addresses the puzzling question of why such projects are started in the first place if it should be clear to at least some of the stakeholders that there is no realistic chance of success. As it turns out, the reasons are very often political.

A typical case is a stakeholder who strongly supports a project proposal but is afraid that decision-makers will reject it because the costs are very high. To win approval for the project, the stakeholder might intentionally underestimate its costs, downplay its risks, and exaggerate its benefits. If the decision-makers regard the stakeholder as an expert, they have good reasons to trust the manipulated cost-benefit analysis, and the fraud may well result in the decision to approve the project.

The behavior of the stakeholder in the example meets the criteria for political behavior outlined before. First, the stakeholder uses power based on expert knowledge, which makes others trust the manipulated analysis. Second, the stakeholder uses the power to achieve a goal, which is the approval of the pet project. Third, the goal is controversial, which makes lying necessary.

As its approval is the result of manipulated information, it can be expected that the project will be in trouble later, but by that time, it may be well past the point of no return. Faced with the prospect of a humiliating total loss, many organizations will continue the project, even if the actual costs are much higher than estimated.

The stakeholder who provided the bogus information may face criticism as a result, but the cost-benefit analysis of planned software projects is hardly an exact science. If an estimate turns out to be wrong, it is usually not difficult to invent reasons later that sound plausible and innocent to explain why the analysis went wrong. In this way, it may be possible to disguise the deceit as an unfortunate, innocent mistake.

The example illustrates how competition for the limited resources of an organization can give rise to political behavior of a stakeholder. Understandably, stakeholders tend to favor causes that benefit themselves rather than others, and they routinely use their power and engage in political behavior to get what they want. As other stakeholders compete for the same resources, conflicts arise, and political processes take place.

Many members of organizations find the use of lies to get a pet project approved morally unacceptable. Therefore, this kind of political behavior has contributed to a bad image of organizational politics, which is commonly associated with dishonesty, infighting, backstabbing, and the use of dirty tricks.

While the disdain for dirty politics is understandable, it is equally important to acknowledge the beneficial functions of political processes in organizations. They can also be thought of as arenas where stakeholders with conflicting goals can argue, persuade, negotiate, bargain, and cooperate to address conflicts and find agreements that reconcile differences constructively. In organizations, this regularly happens in an entirely civilized manner, and it helps find necessary solutions to disagreements that are simply a natural part of organizational life.

Political behavior occurs at any level of authority in organizations, and one of the root causes is that most organizations reward individuals based on their perceived performance. The goal is to encourage superior performance through internal competition, and a natural effect of this approach is that ambitious individuals engage in political behavior to obtain rewards and further their careers. Often this happens at the expense of others, and it can easily lead to situations where working against a colleague is more conducive to career progression than cooperation.

At the same time, organizations heavily depend on cooperation, and members need to appear cooperative to be considered for rewards. To reconcile the conflicting demands, some carefully create the impression that they are cooperative while they secretly undermine the work of others they regard as competitors.

Further evidence for the pervasiveness of political behavior in software development is found in Martin (2020). In his book, Martin identifies some current trends in agile software development that he finds worrying. One of them is the increasing emphasis on agile coaches and their resulting power over software development teams and their processes, which appears to conflict with some core tenets of agile software development.

Martin identifies several reasons for this concerning trend. One is an influential training industry, which stresses the importance of coaching to sell training and certifications. Another is the constant need for coaches in organizations to prove that they are indeed needed, not least to secure their jobs and further their careers. An effective way for them to do it is to disempower development teams and make them dependent on coaches. Martin's observations suggest that cases of this kind are all but rare.

It would be too easy to dismiss all such cases as unintended deviations from the right course, which can be avoided through more sophisticated processes or more training for coaches and other project stakeholders. None of these measures can fundamentally change the fact that organizations are also places where stakeholders compete for rewards. For example, for ambitious agile coaches who focus on their careers, there will always be a temptation to highlight and expand their role at the expense of the teams they coach. If coaches act in this way to advance their interests, they engage in political behavior.

In general, the widespread competition within organizations for recognition, status, power, privileges, perks, promotions, money, and other rewards encourages political behavior. Since it is a well-known, important part of organizational life, it has been extensively studied by management scholars as well as practitioners, resulting in a large number of publications on organizational politics.

Software development offers many opportunities for political behavior and has some specific characteristics that encourage it. For this reason, one would expect organizational politics to be a subject in books on the management of software development. Contrary to this expectation, it is covered in very few titles, and only Yourdon (2003) focuses on the subject.

While many authors on software development have described behavior that is clearly political, very few have linked their observations to the literature on organizational politics. As a result, they treat political behavior as individual mistakes that can be avoided through training rather than an unavoidable, natural aspect of organizations. Because of this narrow perspective, much of the literature in the field explains in detail how things should ideally be done but fails to acknowledge that in practice, there are often political reasons why these prescriptions do not always work as intended. This blind spot has led to a significant gap in the literature.

The present book is an attempt to fill the gap in an engaging and credible way. It is written for stakeholders in software development and provides them with an overview of political behavior and organizational politics. While political actors are usually careful to hide their true intentions and disguise their actions, the goal of the book is to make it easier for stakeholders to identify, analyze, and understand political activities in their projects and organizations.

A large number of popular books on office politics shows that many professionals regard political skills as helpful. Decades of research confirm their view and have contributed to a large body of literature on organizational politics available today. It is a valuable resource for anybody interested in the subject, and one goal of this book is to give readers an overview of some relevant literature suitable for further study. To this end, we provide citations in the text where possible.

The book consists of three main parts. Part I constitutes a concise overview of some key concepts related to power and conflict in organizations. Most of the material presented in the first part is general in nature and not specific to software development. Part II is concerned with software development processes. To a large degree, they define the power balance between project stakeholders, and the focus in this part is on how their design reflects stakeholder interests. Part III of the book looks at the skills that characterize successful political actors. While they usually attempt to hide or disguise their political activities, we highlight them in this part and explain how political behavior works.

Power and Conflict

Fundamental Concepts

A meaningful discussion of organizational politics requires a good understanding of some fundamental concepts. The definitions and explanations offered in this chapter clarify their meaning in the context of this book.

Stakeholder

The term "stakeholder" is central to the study of organizational politics and many other subjects. It was already casually used in the introduction to denote participants of political processes. The stakeholders in a political process are the parties that are affected by it or its outcome. They do not necessarily have substantial power in the process, although in practice, they are typically able to influence it to some degree (Yourdon 2003, p. 49).

It is sometimes best to conceptualize a group of individuals in an organization that share similar interests and cooperate to achieve them as a single stakeholder. Accordingly, a stakeholder can either represent an individual or a group of individuals.

There is no single, correct definition of stakeholders in most practical cases. Instead, any choice of stakeholders is a matter of judgement, represents a particular perspective, and serves a specific purpose. It usually also requires

P. Wendorff, *Politics in Software Development*,
https://doi.org/10.1007/978-1-4842-7380-7_1

trade-offs, and in some situations, it may be better to regard a group of individuals as a single stakeholder, and in others, it may be better to divide the group up into two or more stakeholders. In any case, a stakeholder representing multiple individuals should always be a meaningful unit of people who cooperate to achieve shared goals.

For the analysis of generic management processes in organizations, it is often sufficient to consider only two abstract stakeholders, managers and subordinates. Likewise, it may suffice to distinguish project managers and developers to analyze the interactions within software project teams. However, if the developers have different roles, it may be necessary to define more stakeholders to represent differences in interests or activities. Moreover, additional stakeholders become necessary if their interactions with teams or their members are of interest.

The members of an organization are the individuals who join it, contribute to its operations, and are subject to its rules. All employees are members of their organizations. In this book, we focus on internal stakeholders, which consist of members only.

Goal

Organizations exist to achieve goals. A goal of an organization is something that it tries to accomplish in the future, and it also represents a commitment to use the organization's resources for the purpose. Organizational goals can exist at different levels, for example, strategic or operational, and they can be more or less formal, for example, explicitly stated in official documents or just implied.

The various goals of an organization also compete with another for the available resources. As the resources are limited, it is not possible to maximize goals such as profitability and staff welfare at the same time. Thus, organizational goals also impact the distribution of benefits among stakeholders, which is a major cause of disagreement. While disagreement among stakeholders is nothing unusual, most organizations achieve broad consensus among their most important stakeholders to support their goals.

To encourage support for their goals, organizations usually provide benefits to stakeholders in exchange for cooperation. The best-known of these benefits is the payment of salaries, wages, and bonuses to their members. While these incentives encourage compliant behavior of stakeholders, the availability of resources limits their use, and often their effectiveness declines the more they are provided.

Incentives, punishments, and other means that organizations can use to encourage compliance with their goals have limits. There are always situations where stakeholders engage in the pursuit of goals that are not fully compliant. It means that the goals of organizations and their stakeholders usually differ, although often, there is considerable overlap as well.

There are many reasons why stakeholders hide some of their goals. One is that they are often, at least to some degree, self-serving, which is frowned upon in most organizations. Another is that they compete with others and try to mislead them to gain an advantage. It is therefore common for stakeholders to purposely make misleading statements about their goals in public. Usually, the stated goals sound more acceptable because they better align with organizational goals or are less threatening to other stakeholders. Often the old adage applies that there are always two truths: one that sounds good and another one that is true.

When stakeholders exert influence in political processes, they usually expect opposition from others and anticipate their reactions to make their own political actions more effective. It is a difficult task because they at most know the stated goals of other stakeholders, which may differ a lot from their actual ones. It inevitably adds a third set of goals, which are the perceived goals that one stakeholder ascribes to another. As a political actor does not know the actual goals of other stakeholders and cannot tell in how far stated goals are genuine, political behavior is inevitably based on perceived goals.

To avoid confusion, we use the following convention in this book: Where we refer to stated or perceived stakeholder goals, we will make it explicit, and where we refer to stakeholder goals without qualification, we mean actual goals.

Conflict

The term "conflict" can be confusing because it has two closely related but different meanings. The first meaning of the term describes a goal conflict, which is a state of affairs where the stakeholders in an issue have incompatible goals that cannot be satisfied simultaneously. The second meaning describes a conflict process, which develops when stakeholders act to achieve their goals and try to resolve goal conflicts more or less amicably.

The two meanings of the term are closely related. If a goal conflict occurs, the stakeholders can deal with it in two fundamentally different ways: They can ignore it, either temporarily or permanently, or initiate a conflict resolution process.

Power

As already noted in the introduction, the power of individuals in organizations derives from various factors. Their positions, which give them status and formal authority, are the most visible base of power, but there are other potent bases like expert knowledge or relationships.

The degree of power individuals enjoy may be hard to assess because part of it remains invisible until they use it. Relationships are a case in question because a friendship with an influential colleague may afford considerable leverage in a political struggle but only if the person is willing to get involved. Whether the colleague decides to become active depends on subjective, situational judgements that can be hard to predict.

It follows that the power of individuals is not absolute but can very much depend on the situation. How much power they enjoy only becomes clear when they try to use it, which usually happens when they participate in conflicts. When they engage in them, they try to achieve their goals and use their power to overcome opposition. It suggests the intuitive and simple definition that the power of stakeholders in a given situation is the degree to which they can achieve their own goals that conflict with the goals of other stakeholders.

This definition is indeed adopted by many writers on management, for example, Pfeffer (1994, p. 30). It offers a way to assess the power of stakeholders, but for observers in practice, it is not always easy to apply. An obvious problem is the need to know actual instead of stated goals, which is ultimately impossible.

Another fundamental problem is the question of causality. Assumed, an observer looks at a contested issue in an organization and notes that it is finally resolved in line with the goals of a particular stakeholder. From the coincidence alone, it does not follow that the stakeholder had power and caused the outcome. Instead, it could be that other stakeholders caused it.

Clegg (1989) provides a comprehensive discussion of these and other problems that arise from attempts to define the concept of stakeholder power. It turns out that any known attempt to capture its essence has significant weaknesses. In this light, we adopt the above definition of power in this book. Despite its shortcomings, it provides a simple, intuitive, and essentially adequate idea of what stakeholder power is. We will present more details on the subject in later chapters.

Political Behavior

In this book, we adopt the following definition, which broadly agrees with the one offered by Pfeffer (1994, p. 30) as well as many other writers on management: The behavior of stakeholders is political if they use power to achieve own goals that conflict with the perceived goals of other stakeholders.

The definition does not include an important qualification because it is taken for granted throughout the book: Political behavior in an organization must be legal. As a result, bullying, harassment, the threat of physical violence, and other unacceptable forms of conduct do not qualify as political behavior.

Most behavior in organizations is not political because the stakeholders agree on the required outcomes and how to achieve them. As there are no conflicting goals in these cases, there is no need for any party to resort to power, and consequently, no significant political behavior takes place.

Situations where the goals of stakeholders conflict frequently occur in organizations as well, and therefore some degree of political activity is almost always present in them. In these situations, stakeholders often resort to political behavior to overcome opposition and use whatever power they have to influence outcomes in line with their goals.

As Buchanan and Badham (2020, pp. 41) note, organizational politics tends to have a rather negative image. One reason is that it is often the result of competition among stakeholders who pursue self-serving goals and use unfair means to achieve them. While this is often the case, it is not necessarily so, and political behavior can be the most effective means to achieve legitimate ends. It leads Buchanan and Badham to conclude that the skillful use of political behavior can benefit individuals and organizations. For this reason, the above definition of political behavior represents a neutral position, and there is no suggestion that political behavior in organizations is necessarily bad.

Political Process

The political behavior of stakeholders affects others, which frequently respond with the same kind of behavior when they become aware of it. A political process is the interrelated political behavior of stakeholders targeting a contentious issue. The most prominent type of political process is decision-making. Stakeholders frequently pursue conflicting goals in decision processes and routinely use political behavior to promote their preferred outcomes.

In this sense, a political process can be thought of as an informal arena where stakeholders can engage with one another to resolve a contested issue. It gives stakeholders a space where they can argue, persuade, negotiate, bargain, and cooperate. They can present their positions and challenge those of others, which ideally leads to a competition of ideas and better solutions. In organizations, conflict resolution through political processes regularly happens in an entirely civilized manner, and it helps find necessary solutions to disagreements that are simply a natural part of organizational life.

Political Tactic

A political tactic is a type of basic political behavior that stakeholders use in political processes to achieve their goals. At a minimum, the definition of a tactic describes the type of action necessary to apply it and the intended effect on the target stakeholders.

Maybe the most frequently used political tactic is to manipulate the information available to stakeholders. When political actors put the tactic into practice, they purposely suppress, filter, delay, distort, leak, and invent information. To the extent the manipulated information allows to control other stakeholders, the effect can give political actors an advantage in political processes.

Lists of common political tactics are included in many books, but often the authors use more or less different terms and descriptions. How tactics are defined depends on their purpose and is also a matter of judgement. Their definitions can be more or less specific, and lists of tactics can be more or less detailed and complete.

A short look at some sources illustrates the variety of terms and definitions in use. Buchanan and Badham (2020, p. 269) call the above tactic "information games," while Rollinson (2008, pp. 409) divides it up into two tactics, which he calls "control of information" and "dominate information flows." Handy (1999, p. 307) also divides it up, but he names the two items "information control" and "information distortion."

One reason for different definitions is that an author may want to emphasize a particular aspect. It is the reason why Handy differentiates between the control and distortion of information. He wants to stress that the former, withholding information, is substantially different from the latter, misrepresenting information.

If the use of different terms for similar political tactics is ignored, there is substantial similarity between most lists of common political tactics, but they are far from identical. At present, no single, comprehensive, generally accepted list of political tactics exists in the management literature.

Political Strategy

A political strategy is a plan that coordinates political tactics to achieve important, long-term goals. The most relevant point of the definition is that a strategy is composed of tactics, which implies that the former requires the latter and is more complex.

When stakeholders engage in political processes, their strategies inevitably clash. Because the moves of stakeholders are usually difficult to predict with any degree of certainty, the possibility to plan strategies in advance is often severely limited. In practice, stakeholders frequently revise them, and they emerge from the process as a combination of planned and improvised elements.

Because it is effectively impossible to plan them in advance, the management literature does not offer a comprehensive, generally accepted list of possible political strategies. For the same reason, but also because there is no consensus about political tactics, no generally accepted strategy formulation framework exists.

Perspectives on Power

As power plays a central role in human life, inside and outside of organizations, it is not surprising that it has been extensively studied and debated for centuries. These efforts have not resulted in a single, generally accepted definition of the concept. Instead, different ways to approach the subject have emerged, which highlight certain aspects of power. This chapter presents some of the theoretical perspectives that are relevant to the study of organizational politics.

Unitarism

It is plausible to assume that an organization's paid members have an interest in its success so that their jobs are safe and there is scope for better pay. Of course, there are also non-financial reasons to support organizations, for example, interesting work or an attractive mission. Therefore, it appears reasonable to expect that, in general, the members of organizations support them, not least for their own welfare. If they generally support their organizations, they should accept their goals, structures, and managers as legitimate means for running them and collaborate to achieve success together. This view of organizations as places where people collaborate to pursue shared goals is known as the unitary perspective on power in organizations.

© Peter Wendorff 2022
P. Wendorff, *Politics in Software Development*,
https://doi.org/10.1007/978-1-4842-7380-7_2

While harmony should be the dominant state in organizations from a unitary point of view, it allows for conflict as an exception. If it occurs, it is thought of as a rare, undesirable deviation from the normal, correct state of affairs, which requires corrective action. As there is an assumption that all parties pursue the same goals and are willing to collaborate to achieve them, proponents of unitarism believe that it is in principle possible to resolve most conflicts without much acrimony. Open and honest communication is seen as critical in this process because it helps to share and align different viewpoints. The hope is that once the different standpoints have sufficiently converged, agreement about the best way forward naturally emerges and makes consensus possible, ideally in the form of win-win solutions.

The unitary perspective on power in organizations is popular with managers, as Rollinson (2008, p. 415) points out. It is not surprising because it implies that their subordinates should, at least in general, support them and not challenge their power. In such a climate, managers can give orders and trust them to flow down the organizational hierarchy with minimal friction, distortion, and resistance. For managers, this state of affairs is naturally an attractive proposition.

While the unitary perspective makes the life of managers easier, it may to a degree be wishful thinking on their part in relation to their subordinates. If subordinates disagree with superiors, there may be good reasons for them to stay silent. One is fear to appear as troublemakers, and another is the expectation that their concerns would not be taken seriously. Where subordinates choose to remain silent, it creates the appearance of overall consensus, but it does not mean that conflict is absent. Instead, the silence may only indicate that subordinates are too afraid or frustrated to say what they really think.

The assumptions of unitarism suggest that political behavior in organizations is a rare phenomenon. The reason is that political behavior usually only occurs if there is substantial disagreement over organizational goals, which can hardly happen if all affected stakeholders share the same goals and collaborate to reach them. Even if a political process unfolds, the assumption is that it occurs because of misunderstandings rather than fundamental disagreements and that open and honest communication is the best way to settle the issue amicably.

The literature on the management of software development takes an almost exclusively unitary stance. An anecdote presented by Ripley and Miller (2020, pp. 131) is used in the following as an example to illustrate how authors promote the unitary perspective.

The story took place at a company where managers became concerned about the low productivity of its software development activities. The company's management contracted Miller to find out why the actual productivity was poor when, at least on paper, everything looked just perfect.

Miller's first step was to speak to all stakeholders, in particular, managers and developers. The conversations quickly allowed the conclusion that unreasonable expectations and poor communication had resulted in distrust between developers and managers. Developers would sometimes even fabricate numbers to hide problems with a project from managers. Managers became suspicious, no longer trusted the data and believed that they were told lies. Miller then worked with all stakeholders to build mutual trust and resolve misunderstandings, and the story had a happy ending where everybody was better off.

The anecdote bears many characteristics of the unitary point of view. First, it takes for granted that productivity is a dominant goal shared by all stakeholders. Second, the consultant brought in by management is accepted and trusted by all stakeholders. Third, the problems are essentially the result of misunderstandings, which the parties, albeit with the help of a consultant, can resolve through open and honest communication. Fourth, all stakeholders work together to address the problems, and the story ends with a win-win solution.

While a single anecdote in itself is not remarkable, it is remarkable that Ripley and Miller and countless other authors manage to write whole books that take the unitary perspective for granted. While the rosy picture they convey is likely to please readers who look for easy solutions, one may wonder whether the reality of software professionals in organizations is indeed that rosy.

Pluralism

The assumptions of unitarism project a more harmonious image of organizations than is usually found in reality. While most members of organizations support them to a considerable degree, they usually also pursue their own interests at work, which can easily conflict with those of others or the organizations.

The pluralist perspective on power in organizations is more realistic about the possibility of conflict. While it accepts the essential role of common goals, it recognizes that stakeholders also pursue other goals in organizations. They are often self-serving and create goal conflicts, but they exist for good reasons, and no amount of wishful thinking or open and honest communication can make them disappear.

Maybe the most prominent area where conflicting goals in organizations regularly surface is the distribution of rewards, for example, status, power, privileges, perks, promotions, and money. They are inevitably limited because organizations have limited resources, and their distribution is often a zero-sum game, which means that the win of one stakeholder effectively causes the loss of another.

The fair distribution of rewards in organizations features prominently in virtually all of the countless self-help books on office politics, and the message in them for readers is clear: In many instances, they will have to compete with others to get a fair share of the available rewards. To this end, the books provide plenty of advice on how to win at office politics. The continuing popularity of this kind of literature provides ample evidence that the unitary view of power in organizations is over-optimistic.

The admission that organizations are also places where stakeholders compete for rewards and that this often involves the use of political behavior broadens the view of power in organizations. Where the unitary perspective limits attention to managers and their formal authority, the pluralist perspective acknowledges that all stakeholders can, at least to some extent, develop influence in organizations. While managers have formal authority over subordinates, subordinates can sometimes gain considerable informal power over their managers. It is often the case where individuals control critical information flows on which their superiors depend. The increased attention to informal power raises the question of how it can be acquired and deployed.

Political processes are the way how conflicting stakeholder interests usually play out in organizations. They involve various stakeholders that use their power to achieve organizational but also other, potentially opposed goals. It follows that the processes and their outcomes are not necessarily in the interest of the organizations. Instead, they can go wrong and cause harm, which explains why the pluralist position stresses the need for organizations to establish effective mechanisms for conflict resolution.

Many management scholars believe that the pluralist perspective provides a more realistic description of most organizations than unitarism, Rollinson (2008, p. 415) notes. For managers, it means that they can no longer take it for granted that subordinates will obediently carry out orders. Instead, they have to expect challenges to their authority, and their instructions may be subject to considerable scrutiny, criticism, resistance, and distortion.

As this book is primarily concerned with the analysis of political behavior, it firmly embraces the pluralist perspective on power in organizations. This perspective helps to improve our understanding of software development in the real world. Pluralist assumptions are instrumental in highlighting and investigating many of the issues raised in the book. While we only explain unitarism and pluralism, it is noteworthy that they are not the only plausible perspectives on power. Two alternatives that Rollinson (2008, pp. 415) describes are the radical and the interactionist perspectives.

In the large majority of books on the management of software development, the pluralist perspective on power in organizations plays no significant role. Arguably, despite its age, the best-known exception is still Yourdon's (2003) title *Death March*.

Yourdon defines a project that is so under-resourced that it has almost no chance of success as a "death march" project. Software developers involved in such projects can expect an unpleasant and stressful experience. When the projects finally fail, part of the blame will inevitably go to the developers, even if the failure is not their fault, which creates a substantial risk of unfair reputational damage. Of course, a death march project can result from mere incompetence, but Yourdon (pp. 6) also gives less innocent explanations like power struggles between ambitious managers.

The decisive point Yourdon makes is that managers and other stakeholders sometimes have an incentive not to be open, honest, and cooperative. He concludes that political behavior in organizations is to be expected (p. 77): "Political games something are [sic] we have to accept as an unavoidable phenomenon and cope with them as best we can." This view fundamentally contradicts the unitary perspective on power and suggests that the pluralist perspective is more realistic. Accordingly, the purpose of Yourdon's book is to help his readers cope with politics in death march projects.

Bases of Power

Pluralism assumes that the stakeholders in an organization do not necessarily agree on goals and regularly try to advance their interests. They need power for this purpose, which raises the question of what its bases in organizations are. An academic paper published in 1959 by two American psychologists, John French and Bertram Raven, has been very influential in this respect. In their paper, the authors identify five fundamental bases of power in interpersonal relationships.

They analyze the bases of power in the context of general social relationships between two individuals. It is straightforward to apply their work to power relationships in organizations. The following description of four bases of individual power in organizations summarizes Handy's (1999, pp. 125) adaptation of French and Raven's work.

The four bases of power are:

- Positions
- Expert knowledge
- Resources
- Personal characteristics

Positions in organizations define rights and duties, which gives organizational members position power. It is essentially the formal authority they need to execute their work, and it includes the right to instruct subordinates, the right to use organizational resources, and the right to make decisions. The terms "legal" or "legitimate" power are often used for it as well to emphasize that it derives from official rights that organizations enforce internally.

Expert knowledge is a power base in organizations because they usually try to conduct decision processes and other activities in a rational manner or at least pretend to do so. Rationality requires using relevant expert knowledge where possible. It gives experts power because they provide much of the information that influences decisions and other outcomes of organizational processes.

Because rational organizations highly value expert knowledge, it is the socially most respected base of power in them. As a consequence, there is usually little resistance to influence derived from expertise. However, knowledge is only a dependable base of power if those over whom influence is exercised cooperate and accept it as relevant and valid. Until that happens, claims to expertise rarely result in significant expert power.

Resources are a highly relevant base of power in organizations. They can be material, which means that they have a physical presence, financial, including money and its equivalents, or immaterial like rights, information, or a network of contacts. Mere access to a resource gives resource power, but a much more advantageous position is control. Control over a resource allows to act as a gatekeeper. The gatekeeper metaphor refers to an agent in control of the "gate" between a resource and those who need it, giving the agent the power to decide who gets access and who does not.

Managers with the right to allocate resources are a case where control over resources results in substantial power. They routinely use resources as rewards for subordinates to encourage compliant behavior. The list of possible resources includes highly valued advantages such as pay increases and a better office. The more desirable the resources are in the eyes of their subordinates, the more resource power managers enjoy. Because it rests on rewards, French and Raven coined the term "reward power" for this case, as Handy (1999, p. 127) remarks.

Access to or control over resources in organizations is in many cases a direct consequence of position power and heavily regulated. However, it is not always formally assigned based on positions. In particular, the producer of an immaterial resource like information naturally has access to it and also some control over it. In this sense, Handy (1999, p. 132) observes, all subordinates are gatekeepers to their bosses. It can give them some power over their managers, which the latter usually view with some suspicion. Software developers who implement critical, complex code and keep relevant information secret are a case in question. It can make them indispensable, which improves their bargaining position in political processes like salary negotiations.

Personal characteristics include physical properties, intellectual abilities, and personality traits. They can be a strong base of power if they create feelings in others like admiration, respect, loyalty, or trust. Positive emotions like these make it easier to influence the behavior of individuals. Especially in cases where cooperation from others is needed, they are much more likely to comply and make a genuine effort if they have positive feelings toward the person asking for help. As a base of power, personal characteristics, similar to expert knowledge, are only effective if the target persons cooperate and grant the power. One name for it is "personal power," but it is also frequently referred to as "referent power" or "charisma."

It is noteworthy that Handy (1999, pp. 126) includes physical strength as a fifth base of power. It not only plays a role in some manual professions, but it also matters in situations like bullying where there can be a threat of physical violence. Because we are mainly interested in software development and rule out any illegal application of power, we do not add physical strength to our list and limit it to four bases. It does not mean that physical strength is irrelevant, but there is no need for a dedicated item, and instead, we regard it as a physical property.

The identification of different bases of power highlights the role of informal power in organizations. It is the power of stakeholders beyond their formal authority. Its existence is particularly relevant from a pluralist perspective because it suggests that all stakeholders in organizations can, at least in principle, have power and use it to pursue their goals.

Dimensions of Power

The concept of power is central to the study of human society as well as organizations. It underwent a fundamental evolution in the second half of the 20th century, which took place in three stages. Each of the stages emphasized a particular type of power, and the resulting three-dimensional construct constitutes a valuable, integrative perspective on the concept of power. While much of the original research focused on stakeholders in public administration, the three dimensions are also applicable to power in organizations. Because Clegg (1989) offers a comprehensive discussion of this evolution and its historical context, we only give a short characterization of the three dimensions in the following.

The first dimension of power, which was suggested in the year 1957 by the American academic Robert Dahl, defines the power relationship between two individuals in this way: "A has power over B to the extent that he [sic] can get B to do something B would not otherwise do" (Dahl cited in Clegg 1989, p. 51).

It is straightforward to apply the definition to the four bases of power described in the previous section. For example, it captures situations well where a manager uses formal authority and instructs a subordinate to carry out a task or an individual uses expert power to convince another of a better solution to a problem. In these instances, an individual interacts with another and uses power to make the other person behave in a certain way.

While the first dimension of power certainly captures a lot of the essence of power in organizations, there is an aspect that it does not consider. Organizations represent formal structures that their members have to respect, for example, rules and procedures, and these structures can fundamentally restrict the freedom of members to act. It shows that power in organizations is not only a property of the relationship between an A and a B but that it is also embedded in the organizational environment in which A and B operate.

It leads to the second dimension of power, which the two American academics Peter Bachrach and Morton Baratz suggested in the year 1962, for which they also coined the term "non-decision-making." It represents situations where "an A devotes his [sic] energies to creating [...] institutional practices that limit the scope of the political process to [...] issues that are comparatively innocuous to A" (Bachrach & Baratz cited in Clegg 1989, p. 76).

The second dimension of power recognizes that the stakeholder interests in a political process do not necessarily receive equal attention. Sometimes, stakeholders fail to win attention for their concerns. It gives rise to an important concept called the "organizational agenda." It is the list of critical issues affecting an organization that its decision-makers regard as worthy of attention and debate to prepare decisions. It determines what counts as a relevant decision topic. Stakeholder concerns that never make it on the agenda usually never reach the decision stage either and are more or less ignored.

Control over the agenda is a powerful political weapon in organizations. A stakeholder A has power over a stakeholder B if A can establish practices that shape the agenda of organizations to exclude issues that are important to B but unwanted by A. It means that possible decision alternatives are not even considered, hence the term "non-decision-making." The reference to institutional practices draws attention to the rules of the game embedded in organizations and emphasizes that they are not neutral. On the contrary, those who make the rules likely use them to limit the organizational agenda to their own advantage. In particular, they will usually try to keep anything off it that might seriously challenge their power.

The second dimension of power begs the question of why B would allow A to shape the political agenda to the detriment of B's interests. Clegg (1989, p. 77) offers three simple explanations of how it can happen. First, A may try to frustrate B with endless procrastination, bureaucratic obstacles, phony pretexts, and other destructive political maneuvers until B finally has enough and gives up. Second, B may anticipate that A will oppose an issue, assess the chance to succeed and the likely costs, conclude that it is not worth the effort and decide not to raise it. Third, B may not even consider raising an issue if A is opposed to it, much more powerful than B and highly likely to suppress it.

A comparison of the two dimensions of power in the context of organizations reveals a crucial difference. While the first applies to all members of an organization, the second only applies to those who can create institutional practices and force them on others. In practice, the second dimension describes an application of power that is mainly an option for managers. For example, they can organize work in a way that excludes their subordinates from critical information. As a result, the subordinates may be unable to voice ideas or concerns, which helps to limit decisions and other political processes to the agendas their managers prefer.

In addition to the first and second dimensions of power, the British academic Steven Lukes suggested a third in 1974. The third dimension represents cases where the wants of Bs "may themselves be a product of a system which works against their interests, and in such cases, relates the latter to what they would want and prefer, were they able to make the choice" (Lukes cited in Clegg 1989, p. 92).

In essence, the third dimension of power states that a stakeholder A has power over a stakeholder B if A can influence B's preferences in ways favorable to A. In the context of political processes, the third dimension revisits the notion of stakeholder goals and points out that they are not solely the result of free will. Instead, they are also a product of the environment. For example, they can result from the influence of other stakeholders.

Why does B not rebel against a system that shapes B's preferences to A's advantage? In search of an answer, it is instructive to look at the socialization of individuals in societies. It is an unobtrusive process that imparts societal values and norms to individuals, in particular, while they are young and malleable. The effect of successful socialization is that individuals finally take compliance with the demands of society for granted. Two factors play a critical role in the process and ensure that it rarely causes serious resistance. First, individuals often experience it as a natural part of life rather than something that is forced upon them. Second, noncompliance with the process can result in social exclusion and other forms of punishment.

In the context of organizations, the third dimension describes a more subtle application of power than the second. While the second dimension relies on using administrative measures to keep unwanted issues off the organizational agenda, the third relies on sophisticated psychological effects to prevent members from recognizing them as contentious and debatable. Members are socialized into a way of thinking that makes them overlook the issues or see them as unproblematic, even if it is not in their interest. It requires control of highly complex socialization processes in organizations that, realistically, only managers can achieve. For them, it is an attractive option to gain more power over their subordinates.

The debate about its dimensions illustrates that power in organizations can operate in at least three fundamentally different ways. Even if there is no direct power relationship between stakeholders, it may still exist indirectly through organizational structure or socialization processes.

Latent Conflict

The existence of conflicting goals in organizations is all but inevitable, and for many, there is no easy way to reconcile them. Often there is also no compelling benefit for any stakeholder in addressing the conflicts. Sometimes, the best solution may be to ignore them for the time being, strike an uneasy truce, and "[l]et sleeping dogs lie," as an old adage goes. This pragmatic approach plays a vital role in organizations because stakeholders need to work together regardless of lingering conflicts. In this chapter, we look at some of the ways this is achieved in practice.

Causes of Conflict

Stakeholders in organizations usually pursue common organizational goals, but they also have their own interests. To what extent this leads to conflict is mainly dependent on three factors:

- Personal characteristics
- Organizational structure
- Domain properties

In the following, we shortly describe the three factors.

Some conflicts between individuals in organizations arise from minor disagreements, harmless misunderstandings, accidental misbehavior, or mismatched personalities. Certain attitudes make such problems more likely, and the "poisonous people" to which Fitzpatrick and Collins-Sussman (2015, ch. 4) devote a chapter of their book are a case in question. Poisonous people

P. Wendorff, *Politics in Software Development*,
https://doi.org/10.1007/978-1-4842-7380-7_3

are individuals who, for example, have oversized egos, feel entitled to preferential treatment, make no effort of their own, or waste the time of others. Without a doubt, poor behavior in the workplace is annoying, but it is also relatively easy to deal with as long as it is not malicious and no critical goals are at stake. Usually, it is enough to talk with another or avoid each other to diffuse the situation.

Fair competition in organizations is one thing, but the type of individual that Fitzpatrick and Collins-Sussman (2015, p. 105) label "office politician" is a different story. As Fitzpatrick and Collins-Sussman describe individuals of this type, they tend to have superior people skills, which they relentlessly use to seek their advantage at the expense of others. They are quick at blaming others and like to steal credit, and because they also tend to be highly manipulative, it is dangerous to trust them.

The term "Machiavellianism" denotes extreme cases of this behavior. Robbins and Judge (2019, p. 144) characterize these persons as pragmatic, emotionally distanced, highly manipulative individuals who aggressively pursue their agenda and believe that ends can justify means. They lie, manipulate, betray, and are prepared to do what it takes to get ahead of others and achieve their own goals. If it suits them, they hide or deny the existence of conflict and create a false sense of unity, but that does not stop them from pursuing their hidden agendas when they spot an opportunity to win an advantage.

Machiavellianism is often observed together with two other personality traits that can cause severe conflict in organizations: narcissism and psychopathy. Narcissists show an inflated sense of self-importance and entitlement, and psychopaths show little or no remorse if their actions harm others. Because the three personality traits are often observed together, and their definitions partly overlap, they are collectively called the "Dark Triad" (Robbins & Judge 2019, pp. 144).

The structure of an organization is the relatively stable, official set of features that define what its parts and activities are and how they are related, grouped, coordinated, and controlled to achieve its goals. Hierarchies, positions, departments, teams, roles, rules, procedures, and task definitions are all ele-ments of organizational structure (Rollinson 2008, pp. 502). It follows that software processes used by organizations are a part of their structure specific to software development.

How organizations are structured strongly influences the level of conflict in them. One factor is the division of labor. The structure divides up tasks and allocates them to different stakeholders, which tend to develop their specific perspectives and often prioritize their own goals at the expense of others. Another reason is the distribution of resources. Their structure also influences how organizations distribute their limited resources among their stakeholders, which inevitably creates competition. Because competing stakeholders cause many conflicts in organizations, their reward system is a fundamental conflict management tool, and its design can incentivize cooperation or competition.

Some professional domains are characterized by a clearly defined body of generally accepted knowledge, a strict, regulated system of professional qualifications, and a low rate of change. In fields like accounting and medicine, these conditions more or less apply. Their shared background substantially lowers the chance of disagreement among professionals in these fields. The domain of software development is very different and characterized by a comparatively contested body of knowledge, a wide variety of unregulated professional qualifications, and an extremely high rate of technological change.

Given this state of affairs, it is no surprise that software development provides plenty of opportunity for conflicting opinions about practices, methods, techniques, and tools. The ongoing debate in the last two decades about the advantages and disadvantages of agile software development methods is a prominent example of this potential for disagreement. As Meyer (2014) convincingly shows, there is still substantial controversy on the subject among experts and no consensus in sight.

In summary, it can be concluded that personal characteristics and organizational structure cause conflict in all organizations, but that the relatively high potential for disagreement resulting from domain characteristics sets software development apart.

Stages of Conflict

In Chapter 1, we remarked that the term "conflict" has two different meanings. In the first case, it describes a state of affairs and merely recognizes the existence of conflicting goals. In the second case, the term denotes a process, which starts with a goal conflict and includes the activities of stakeholders addressing it.

A large body of research supports the view of conflict among stakeholders in organizations as a process that develops gradually and goes through certain phases. While different conflict process models have been suggested, there is agreement that a pivotal stage is when the stakeholders use political behavior to achieve their goals. It is when the stakeholders openly engage in a confrontation. Accordingly, Rollinson (2008, p. 420) labels this stage "open conflict," but the term "overt conflict" is also in use and means the same. Open conflict will be the subject of Chapter 4.

Stakeholders usually become active long before a conflict reaches the open stage. Once they notice the possibility of conflicting goals, they first assess how important the issue is to them. Other considerations are the chance to achieve their goals through political action and the associated risks. Based on their assessment of the situation, they decide whether to avoid, delay, or initiate open conflict.

Many of the conflict process models presented in the management literature are rather detailed and include multiple stages. For example, the model that Robbins and Judge (2019, pp. 671) adopt consists of five, of which the fourth is the stage of open conflict. This degree of detail is not necessary for the purpose of this book, and therefore we adopt a much simpler approach, which is comparable to the model presented by Rollinson (2008, pp. 419). Accordingly, we include all activities and events occurring before the open stage in a stage called "latent conflict."

The simple model we use in this book consists of only two stages, latent and open conflict. The start stage is always latent, and the process potentially, but not always, progresses to the open stage. The remainder of the chapter focuses on latent conflict.

Latent conflict is often only a transition phase and can quickly give way to open confrontation. Most of the time, the transition occurs when a stakeholder starts to pursue its goals more aggressively because there is an opportunity to gain from a political process. However, it can also last for extensive periods of time. Possible reasons are that the stakeholders in a contested issue do not regard it as important enough, lack the power for effective political action, or fear retaliation by other stakeholders.

There are, of course, still conflicting goals present in situations of this kind, but if no party is willing to initiate a political process, the conflicts are not addressed. At the same time, they usually also do not go away on their own. For this reason, latent conflict can be more of a temporary, uneasy truce than a stable solution and frequently causes palpable tensions. In an attempt not to exacerbate the tensions, individuals often become very careful about what they say and avoid troublesome topics that might stir up conflict.

Guarded Communication

Most authors on software development emphasize the importance of effective communication among stakeholders and make the point that it should ideally be clear, open, honest, and respectful. It makes most sense if a unitary perspective on power is taken for granted because unitarism describes a scenario where stakeholders have nothing to hide.

From a pluralist perspective on power, things are more complicated. As the pluralist view allows for different, contradictory stakeholder goals, the notion of open and honest communication raises the question of whose interests it would serve in a given situation. In the presence of latent conflict, it is well possible that some stakeholders, if not all, have good reasons to avoid open and honest communication because it could lead to an open confrontation that might harm their interests.

The alternative to open and honest communication is guarded communication, which is an attempt to avoid unwanted consequences by carefully shaping messages based on their expected and desired effects.

It allows people to interact at work even if they mutually dislike one another, have conflicting interests or poorly matched work styles. In organizations, this is essential because their members have to work together, regardless of whether they are a good match or not. In situations where highlighting a controversial issue would do more harm than good, guarded communication can help to keep conflict in the latent state. It may result in a situation that is often metaphorically described as "the elephant in the room," but that is often still better than a potentially destructive open confrontation.

Guarded communication regularly occurs in daily life, for example, when individuals use tactful language, change the topic, or tell white lies to avoid bad feelings, offense, or conflict. Often there is little or no obvious harm in such deviation from openness and honesty, but it can make it easier for people to get along in social situations.

Members of organizations routinely use guarded communication by filtering information to avoid negative consequences or reduce conflict. Subordinates who want to please their superiors and tell them what they want to hear rather than the complete truth are a well-known case in question.

From a unitary perspective, hiding the truth from other members of an organization is usually regarded as unacceptable behavior and a clear sign of serious problems. Pluralism takes a very different view and regards guarded communication in organizations as natural, unavoidable, and sometimes necessary to avoid unproductive open conflict. It does not deny the benefits of open and honest communication in organizations, but it rejects the unitarist claim that it is the only reasonable choice for their members.

Strategic Ambiguity

In the context of organizational communication, the term "strategic ambiguity" is used to denote the deliberate use of ambiguous, vague, or unclear messages for political ends.

Efforts that require support from multiple stakeholders that share some goals but not all are a scenario that frequently leads to strategic ambiguity in organizations. In such a situation, the stakeholders sometimes define goals at a level of abstraction that allows all parties to accept them, while the more controversial details are left to interpretation. The strategic ambiguity allows to avoid disagreement and helps unite the stakeholders, at least for the moment (Eisenberg 1984).

A statement of this kind can create a powerful sense of unity among stakeholders by focusing on what unites them rather than differences. The resulting climate of cooperation can increase the willingness to tolerate latent conflicts, allowing the stakeholders to defer their resolution to later.

Yourdon (2003, p. 183) describes how strategic ambiguity is often used to unite stakeholders in software projects. If the stakeholders are unable to reach an agreement on important points but still want a project to go ahead, they can

> simply "agree to disagree," allowing the project to muddle onward without any documented agreement or approval of these key issues; or the documented version of requirements, interfaces, acceptance criteria, and other issues will be so vague and abstract that the programmers will be forced to "invent" the details for themselves.

The use of strategic ambiguity to hide stakeholder disagreement creates the risk that the differences will prove unresolvable later. While this concern is certainly justified, stakeholders sometimes prefer to ignore it and be optimistic to get projects going. They know that the stakes will be higher later and hope that the increased pressure will force all parties to cooperate and resolve their remaining differences. Another hope is that once the first signs of success appear, everybody will want to look supportive. It is a risky gamble, and the projects have a high chance to end up as death marches.

In the field of software development, the effective use of strategic ambiguity was demonstrated in the year 2001 by a group of 17 authors who created the highly influential Agile Manifesto (Beck et al. 2001). It can serve as an example of a message that was made possible and attractive through the skillful use of strategic ambiguity.

As one of them, Cockburn (2001, p. 215) notes that the authors of the manifesto had rather diverse backgrounds and represented substantially different interests and software development methods. Their differences made agreeing on the contents of the manifesto complicated. Eventually, they managed to agree on four value statements and twelve principles, the Agile Manifesto, which became instrumental in the rise of a powerful movement.

The four value statements express preferences and are rather general, vague, and ambiguous. It has the effect that readers can interpret them in various ways and read their preferred meaning into them. They "are the kinds of statements that everyone can agree with without actually changing anything about the way they work," as Martin (2020, pp. 13) observes, who is another of the manifesto's authors.

Not only did the use of strategic ambiguity help the authors of the manifesto to agree on a common text, despite their differences, but it has also made it easier for readers to identify with it. Since its publication, the Agile Manifesto has proven to be highly influential, which allows the conclusion that its strategic ambiguity was no serious impediment to its effectiveness.

Another powerful effect of strategic ambiguity is to create the conditions for plausible deniability in case messages attract criticism. Often producers of messages can conveniently claim that the criticism results from a misunderstanding of what they truly mean. This ability to deny responsibility makes it less risky for stakeholders to endorse potentially controversial messages. If they have unanticipated negative consequences, the stakeholders can adjust their position, save face, avoid accountability, and shift the blame to the recipients of messages (Eisenberg 1984).

Plausible deniability allows stakeholders to emphasize what a message does not mean rather than explaining what it actually is, which shifts the onus and risk of interpretation to its recipients. Meyer's (2014) critical evaluation of the Agile Manifesto shows how plausible deniability shields it from criticism.

As the four value statements in the manifesto are very general, Meyer bases his analysis on his personal, specific, detailed understanding of their meaning. He expresses it in the form of five "general tenets" (p. 2) that he subsequently discusses. As a consequence, an easy way to dismiss his evaluation is to deny that the five general tenets are a fair representation of the value statements in the manifesto. It demonstrates how plausible deniability discourages a critical evaluation of messages and thus protects them from scrutiny.

Open Conflict

Stakeholders with conflicting goals are not always willing to ignore them, and organizations routinely need to deal with this situation. Therefore, a key goal informing the design of organizations is the optimal management of conflict. Any practical solution has limitations, though, which leaves room for the political activities of stakeholders. In this chapter, we have a first look at the role these activities play in the resolution of conflict in organizations.

Allowing Conflict

Latent conflict occurs in organizations if stakeholders choose to ignore their conflicting goals and avoid political behavior that would highlight their differences. It routinely happens and can be highly beneficial, not least to prevent unrest in cases where a confrontation would likely not achieve much good but could degenerate into a pointless or destructive struggle.

While the avoidance of open conflict in organizations reduces the level of unrest in them, it can also result in stagnation. In many situations, it may be convenient to ignore conflicting goals to avoid the possible risk of confrontation, but it hides problems, prevents change, and tends to favor the status quo, even if it is no longer appropriate. Fear of conflict can quickly develop into a problem because all organizations need the ability to adapt, and timely change can be a matter of survival in a competitive environment.

© Peter Wendorff 2022
P. Wendorff, *Politics in Software Development*,
https://doi.org/10.1007/978-1-4842-7380-7_4

Change in organizations is very often the outcome of an ongoing search for improvement and competition of ideas put forward by stakeholders with different viewpoints. Without this competition and the courage to openly disagree, an organization can develop a false sense of security, become complacent, miss opportunities, and decline over time (Handy 1999, pp. 291).

As a result, organizations have an ambivalent relationship with conflict. They need to allow it to some degree to enable the healthy competition of ideas that drives improvement and necessary change. At the same time, they need to harness it to create the unity and stability that are necessary to get routine work done smoothly and efficiently.

While some open conflict in organizations is necessary, it is not always productive. In particular, if it is disruptive, it may be urgent to find a solution that all stakeholders can support. One factor that can make conflict resolution difficult is the behavior of the conflict parties toward another.

Behavior Styles

In Chapter 3, we pointed out that stakeholders usually consider a number of factors before they engage in open conflict. For example, they likely look at the relevance of the issue at stake and the opportunities and risks associated with political action. Based on the assessment, they develop a clearer idea of what they want to accomplish and how they intend to approach the conflict.

The American management scholar Kenneth Thomas developed a simple taxonomy of behavior styles that stakeholders in conflicts can choose, which he published in 1976. It groups conflict behavior along two dimensions. Thomas labeled the first "assertiveness," and it measures the intention of a stakeholder to achieve own goals. The second is "cooperativeness," which measures the willingness to satisfy competing goals of other parties.

The taxonomy is intuitive and straightforward, and there is a substantial body of research to support it. It has become very influential and is covered in many textbooks, for example, Robbins and Judge (2019, p. 673) and Rollinson (2008, pp. 422). The taxonomy defines five groups that characterize the behavior styles of stakeholders that face open conflict. In the following list of the groups, we indicate the associated levels of assertiveness and cooperativeness in brackets:

- Avoiding (low, low)
- Accommodating (low, high)
- Competing (high, low)
- Compromising (medium, medium)
- Collaborating (high, high)

A stakeholder choosing an avoiding style tries to keep a conflict latent and avoid escalation to open conflict. It often involves withdrawal from a conflict situation, for example, by avoiding contact with the other parties. Avoidance may be an attractive option if a disagreement is unimportant, and it is easier to live with it than bring about a resolution.

An accommodating style means that a stakeholder is willing to surrender and prioritizes the interests of the other parties over its own. An accommodating style can be motivated by several considerations. For example, it is probably appropriate if a stakeholder does not care, is simply in the wrong, or has no realistic chance of winning.

A competing style is the opposite of accommodation and means that a stakeholder is determined to win and prioritizes its own interests over those of the other parties. Accordingly, it may be appropriate if vital interests are at stake and there is a realistic chance of winning without intolerable reputational damage.

A compromising style is a middle position between accommodation and competition. It means that a stakeholder wants to avoid an outcome that creates losers and gives equal weight to the concerns of all parties. A compromise may be the best option if the parties have similar levels of power and there is a desire to avoid an unproductive stalemate.

Finally, a collaborating style is an attempt to find a win-win solution. It means that all stakeholders engage in constructive problem-solving and treat each other fairly. Naturally, it is only an option if they all choose the approach, and the nature of the conflict lends itself to a solution that benefits all of them. In many situations, it is not an option because they are essentially zero-sum conflicts.

The behavior styles the parties to a conflict choose have a considerable impact on their ability to settle their differences constructively. Especially if multiple stakeholders choose a competing style, it is inevitably more difficult and time-consuming for them to find common ground. It creates conditions where they can quickly become locked into an unproductive stalemate.

Sometimes, stakeholders enter the negotiation process with a competitive style but later change to a less assertive or more cooperative style to achieve an agreement. While flexibility in style can undoubtedly contribute to conflict resolution, Rollinson (2008, p. 423) cautions that the potential may be limited. Research on personal differences suggests that individuals tend to have a predisposition to approach conflict in specific ways, and their capacity to switch from an unproductive style to a more productive one may be limited. If stakeholders are unable to resolve a conflict, the next step is usually mediation by a higher-level manager.

Resolution by Hierarchy

While the structures of organizations come in various shapes and can be very complex, they are usually a combination of certain basic types. Some of the most widely used are:

- Hierarchy
- Matrix organization
- Bureaucracy
- Team organization

Basic types describe pure, abstract, idealized structures that are mainly useful for theoretical analysis. Their value lies in their simplicity, which allows studying their function, strengths, weaknesses, and other properties in isolation. In the following, we look at hierarchy as an example and outline how it structures formal authority and deals with conflict.

While hierarchy had been used to structure organizations for many centuries before, significant interest in the theoretical analysis of the practice only became visible at the start of the 20th century. The French engineer and manager Henri Fayol was the most notable contributor to these efforts because he seamlessly integrated the subject into a comprehensive, theoretical analysis of management, which became highly influential.

One of Fayol's main concerns was that efficient work organization depends on clarity. Workers should always know what to do and should not have to deal with a lack of direction or confusion caused by multiple superiors giving conflicting instructions. Fayol postulated 14 principles of organizational design, of which the following two are particularly relevant to the goal of clarity:

- The unity of command principle stipulates that every worker should have a single boss
- The scalar chain principle establishes a chain of command between the top management level and any other part of the organization

Together these two principles establish a simple hierarchy with different layers of authority. In normal circumstances, information and instructions flow along the chain of command without skipping levels.

Hierarchy is widely used in organizational design. For example, in software development, many projects have a hierarchical structure. A single project manager is typically in charge of smaller ones, while bigger ones are subdivided into a hierarchy of smaller subprojects. This setup centralizes authority in the project managers, and they are authorized and responsible to deal with most issues arising from their projects.

A hierarchical organizational structure establishes a simple procedure to deal with conflicting goals of stakeholders. If they lack the authority or ability to handle a conflict, they must escalate it to the next higher level in the hierarchy, and the process continues until it reaches a manager with the authority and ability to handle it. The manager then decides the issue, and the necessary instructions are passed down the hierarchy to all affected parts of the organization for implementation.

The formalism to refer issues up and down the organizational hierarchy is based on the assumption that knowledge, experience, and competence increase at a higher level. It means that the more senior managers handle the issues that are more critical, controversial, or complex.

To make good decisions, the managers should ideally follow the rational choice approach to decision-making. It requires them to find all relevant information about the issue at hand, consider all possible alternatives, evaluate their expected consequences, and choose the best option for the organization.

Managerial decision behavior has been the subject of intense research for many decades. It has led to the realization that the high demands of the rational choice approach on the knowledge and cognitive abilities of decision-makers are often not met in practice. For routine decisions in stable and simple situations, it is a plausible model, but for non-routine decisions in complex scenarios, it is unrealistic because its demands are beyond the capabilities of most decision-makers (Rollinson 2008, p. 255).

In reality, decision-makers are rarely able to look at all relevant information. Because managers higher up in the hierarchy are usually farther away from the action, much of the information they need has to be provided by subordinates and other parties. Inevitably, it creates opportunities for political actors to manipulate decisions by hiding, highlighting, or distorting relevant information. In practice, this kind of political behavior routinely occurs in organizations. The consequence is that the resulting decisions are the outcome of political processes and may reflect stakeholder power and political skill much more than facts, rational arguments, and organizational goals.

Resolution by Politics

Conflict resolution by hierarchy regularly involves political processes, but they are not necessarily detrimental. On the contrary, they provide arenas where stakeholders with conflicting goals can argue, persuade, negotiate, bargain, and cooperate to address conflicts. Stakeholders have the opportunity to present their positions and respond to competing viewpoints, which allows them to challenge questionable assumptions and unsubstantiated claims. Ideally, it helps them find fair agreements that take all relevant perspectives into account, reconcile differences constructively, and result in the best possible solutions.

Stakeholder conflicts are simply a natural aspect of organizations, and political processes play a central role in their resolution. Therefore, it is not surprising that organizational politics has been a field of substantial academic research for many decades. One of the most notable contributors to these efforts is the American academic Jeffrey Pfeffer.

Pfeffer's (1981) first book on power in organizations is written for an academic audience and presents a comprehensive analytical framework for organizational politics. He primarily derives the framework from scholarly research, including his own, which he combines with anecdotal and other evidence for illustration.

He published a second book on the same subject in 1992, which became available as paperback edition Pfeffer (1994) two years later. The purpose was to expand on his earlier book but also to make the subject more accessible to a professional audience. Despite its age, the book still represents the most relevant framework for the analysis of organizational politics and has been widely cited in the scholarly literature.

In this section, we only present a first, short overview of Pfeffer's (1994) analytical framework and leave most details to Part III later in the book. In particular, we explain how it relates to the bases of power and the three-dimensional view of power described in Chapter 2.

Unsurprisingly, Pfeffer rejects the unitary view of organizations, which he regards as wishful "New Age thinking" (p. 8). Instead, he sees conflict as a natural part of organizations and organizational politics as what happens in them when there is disagreement about ends or means. In his eyes, mastering politics in organizations is one of the skills that make managers successful. It is the ability to get things done despite opposition, and his book is an attempt to provide an accessible, credible, practical introduction to the subject for professionals.

Pfeffer describes several political tactics, which fall into two categories. In part II of his book, he focuses on the bases of power that we shortly described in Chapter 2 and provides detailed information on how members of organizations can systematically develop them to increase their power. In part III, he describes strategies and tactics that use existing power to achieve various goals.

Most of the tactics described in part III of Pfeffer's book refer to the first dimension of power. An example is chapter 13, in which he looks at the politics of information and explains various ways how political actors routinely manipulate it to influence decisions. However, chapters 14 and 15 are notable exceptions because they refer to the second and third dimension and describe the exercise of power through organizational structure and symbolic action.

The formal structure of organizations has many functions. One is to organize their activities efficiently, but the other is to assign power to stakeholders. For example, hierarchies, positions, roles, policies, rules, and procedures are elements of their structure. They define the level of formal authority that organizational members have and to what extent they can participate in decisions and other political processes.

Pfeffer rightly claims that organizational structure is not purely motivated by a desire to maximize efficiency. Instead, at least in part, it needs to be understood as the result of power as well as an instrument of power. Managers in organizations use it to maintain, reinforce, and exercise their power. They decide the distribution of formal authority among the stakeholders and which parties participate in political processes. By admitting or excluding specific stakeholders, they determine which interests the organizational agenda represents. In this respect, the structures created by managers in organizations represent the second dimension of power.

Symbolic action is a management technique that appeals to the emotional side of organizational members. Its purpose is to influence their feelings toward their work and organizations. Symbolic action usually relies on subliminal psychological effects that feel normal to individuals to avoid the appearance of manipulation. As a consequence, the target persons often do not fully notice the influence on their behavior.

The use of symbolic action by managers typically involves the creation of specific language, symbols, ceremonies, settings, and other artifacts. They are designed to symbolize and highlight group membership and encourage members to become emotionally attached to their organizations, teams, or work. Managers carefully control group processes to shape the beliefs of the group members and increase their commitment to organizational goals. Because symbolic action ultimately targets changes in the belief systems of individuals, it represents the third dimension of power.

Managers create organizational structure and engage in symbolic action to control the stakeholder activities in organizations indirectly. Of course, they also interact with stakeholders directly. They are privileged because they can rely on all three dimensions of power, whereas most other stakeholders, in particular their subordinates, can usually only rely on the first.

Nevertheless, it is not a foregone conclusion that managers will always prevail in political processes. Their formal authority is a potent form of power, but it is not the only one in organizations. There are other relevant bases of power, and stakeholders can use them to advance their own goals. In reality, managers are not able to make all these unofficial goals disappear, and they cannot stop stakeholders from pursuing them.

Whatever managers do to control stakeholders is never guaranteed to achieve its purpose. The orders they give, the structures they create, and the belief systems they promote represent their power. They serve as the institutional frame in which organizational politics takes place, but they are open to challenge and can become the target of the political behavior of stakeholders with various other agendas.

Software processes are a form of organizational structure specific to software development. Managers establish them to control software development activities in organizations. Because they give more power to some stakeholders than others, the processes are likely controversial and the target of political behavior. At the same time, they create the environment and conditions in which political behavior in software development takes place. In the following Part II of the book, we will have a detailed look at their political nature.

Software Processes

Process Design

Software processes help managers stay in control of software development in organizations. One of their functions is to establish a productive distribution of power among the stakeholders, which naturally reflects the priorities of management. It exposes the processes to political behavior because power is always a controversial topic. In general, software processes have a lot to do with power and politics. In this chapter, we have a closer look at the relationship and the role stakeholders play in it.

Process Industry

The cost-effective development of software is a central concern for many organizations. It has given rise to a lucrative industry around software development processes, which offers consulting, coaching, training, certifications, books, conferences, and tools. Different processes often compete for the same market, which creates enormous pressure to make exaggerated claims about their effectiveness for marketing reasons.

The competition became particularly visible with the publication of the Agile Manifesto in the year 2001, which was a very successful attempt by an alliance of supporters of agile processes to promote them.

Meyer (2014) shows that the proponents of agile processes have made a number of bold claims that were often not backed up by convincing evidence. He presents a thorough discussion of flaws in the arguments of prominent proponents of agile processes, but without a doubt, his observations apply to the entire software process industry.

© Peter Wendorff 2022
P. Wendorff, *Politics in Software Development*,
https://doi.org/10.1007/978-1-4842-7380-7_5

Part of the problem is the difficulty of scholars to gain the kind of access to organizations that is needed for independent, rigorous, empirical research in practice settings. One reason is that research rarely benefits the participating organizations. Another is that the research process is problematic from their perspective. Not only can it disturb their operations, but the publication of results in academic journals can be embarrassing to individuals and organizations. Moreover, the information can also benefit competitors.

Because it is difficult for scholars to gain unfettered access to organizations for the purpose of research, many studies of software development processes are carried out by or with the help of consultants or advocacy organizations. They can sometimes gain access more easily, but they are usually not independent because they have direct or indirect financial interests related to the studies. Meyer (2014, p. 29) certainly has a point when he warns that such studies may suffer from serious methodological flaws and other problems that can render them untrustworthy.

A case study of a software development project presented by Schwaber and Beedle (2001, pp. 26), two consultants, illustrates Meyer's point. The purpose of their book is to describe an agile software development process called "Scrum." From their case study, the authors conclude (p. 30):

> By using Scrum, the team was able to cut through the noise and start delivering valuable product. Time that would have otherwise been wasted was spent working. The team was able to focus itself and deliver product.

The conclusion the authors draw from the case study appears to be that Scrum was the major success factor in it, and it is, of course, consistent with the purpose of their book. Critical readers of the case study may not find this conclusion compelling, though, because the central figure in it is a highly effective team leader who strongly influenced all critical decisions and carefully led his team to success. The team leader was Ken Schwaber, one of the two authors.

Meyer (2014, p. 29) agrees with many other experts that a major success factor of an agile software development team is its leader. Therefore, rather than concluding that Scrum was the main reason for success in the case study, it is equally justifiable to claim that it was the team's skillful leader. Schwaber and Beedle do not mention this rather obvious alternative explanation, and it raises concerns that their analysis is potentially biased in favor of Scrum and not entirely objective.

Poor research and dubious claims related to software processes are not new problems. About two years after the publication of the Agile Manifesto, Boehm and Turner (2003, p. 5) already observed that it had given rise to intense controversy and widespread confusion and that "perhaps some marketing hyperbole" played a role in it. Meyer's (2014) comprehensive analysis about a decade later showed that the problem had not disappeared. On the contrary, Pressman and Maxim (2019, p. 41) recently confirmed that the debate is ongoing and warned that "this methodology debate risks degeneration into a religious war."

Much of the debate sparked by the Agile Manifesto has undoubtedly been fuelled by vested interests that prefer rhetoric over science. Fortunately, scholars and practitioners have also carried out a lot of credible and convincing research on software processes.

Nevertheless, many important questions remain unanswered because high-quality research on the subject is challenging and expensive. Moreover, questionable research exists as well, and not all claims made in the literature are credible. Industrial success stories are often based on selected anecdotes and suffer from conflicts of interest, limiting their credibility. Academic studies are often based on small-scale experiments with students, limiting their generalizability to practice settings (Meyer 2014, pp. 28).

The uncertainty surrounding software processes has the consequence that there are no clear answers to many questions regarding their use in organizations. It leaves considerable room for influential stakeholders to promote processes that serve their specific interests.

Illustrative Processes

Where we refer to specific software development processes in this book, the sole purpose is to illustrate aspects of organizational politics in software development. There is no intention to provide an overview of any process or describe the latest stage in its evolution. We use three processes for illustration throughout the book and present some general background information in this section to avoid repetition. They are:

- Unified Process (UP)
- Extreme Programming (XP)
- Scrum

Together with variants of the waterfall process, these three were dominant in the ten years following the publication of the Agile Manifesto. All four processes are still widely in use at the time of writing, but it is noteworthy that other approaches like Kanban and DevOps (Pressman & Maxim 2019), which play no role in what follows, have recently gained considerable attention too.

We intentionally selected the three processes because of their close historical relationship with the manifesto. Its publication in the year 2001 was a pivotal moment in the history of software development, and the three processes profoundly influenced its spirit. The manifesto had significant technical as well as political ramifications, which provide a particularly suitable context for the exploration and illustration of political aspects of software development.

Unified Process (UP)

Jacobson et al. (1999) describe the Unified Process (UP), which is a comprehensive, generic software development process. The Rational Unified Process (RUP) is a specific, detailed, proprietary variant of the UP and one of the best-known processes.

The UP targets a wide range of project sizes and types. For this reason, the generic process needs to be tailored to a given project. In practice, it means that the UP serves as a process framework, which is usually scaled down to a reduced, specific version that is optimal for a project.

Although the book by Jacobson et al. consists of more than 400 pages of detailed technical explanations, it does not cover the UP completely. Given its size and complexity, tailoring the UP to the needs of a project is a challenging task. In practice, it was often not scaled down enough, and projects frequently used unnecessarily large software development processes based on the UP. It contributed to the widely held perception that the UP encourages "heavyweight" processes, as Larman (2003, p. 192) notes.

Larman (2003, p. 187) claims that the creators of the UP preferred a "relatively light approach to process" but that they did not communicate it well enough. Indeed, Jacobson et al. (1999) do not explain how to tailor the UP to a specific project, which creates the impression that they do not regard it as an essential topic. Instead, they refer to Royce (1998) for further information. While Royce discusses the tailoring of software processes, he does not give special consideration to the UP.

At the time the Agile Manifesto was published, the UP was one of the most widely used and best-documented software process frameworks. A key reason for the manifesto's publication was that "heavyweight" processes like the UP had caused considerable problems and frustration. As an alternative, the manifesto promotes agile processes and defines some of their key characteristics.

When the Agile Manifesto established the term "agile" for the approach to software development it promotes, the search for a suitable counterpart for the properties of more formal processes like the UP, which were not regarded as agile, began. Following Boehm and Turner (2003), we prefer the term "plan-driven" in this book, but it is noteworthy that "predictive" is popular as well.

The distinction of agile versus plan-driven processes is a simplification, of course. As Larman (2003, pp. 192) rightly states, it is possible to tailor the UP with more or less emphasis on agile characteristics. It would therefore be wrong to view agile and plan-driven as two distinct classes of processes, and it is better to view them as endpoints of a continuum.

While it is certainly possible to tailor the UP prioritizing agility, there is no question that Jacobson et al.'s (1999) initial definition of the process framework in no way emphasized this approach. In particular, of the four key attributes of agile processes that Boehm and Turner (2003, p. 17) identify, self-organization and emergence play no significant role in Jacobson et al.'s initial definition. It indicates that there were severe limits to the degree of agility that tailoring could achieve with the initial version of the UP. Boehm and Turner rightly caution that such "lightened" plan-driven processes are not agile processes in the sense of the Agile Manifesto.

It is only natural that after the success of the Agile Manifesto, advocates of the UP began to prefer a more agile interpretation of it, not least for marketing reasons. In this book, we do not pay attention to the evolution of the process and will use its initial definition according to Jacobson et al. (1999), which we regard as an essentially plan-driven approach.

Extreme Programming (XP)

One of the 17 authors of the Agile Manifesto is Kent Beck, and the success of the manifesto drew increased attention to the Extreme Programming (XP) software process (Beck 1999), which he and others had developed and applied in the preceding years.

Compared to the UP, XP targets a much narrower range of project sizes and types. It is a concrete, agile software development process and not a generic framework like the UP. For this reason, it is usually not necessary to tailor the process to specific projects. Larman (2003, p. 141) warns that tailoring is possible but risky because the elements of XP are tightly integrated and work in synergy, which creates a carefully balanced system that modifications can easily disturb.

As the name "Extreme Programming" suggests, the method focuses as far as possible on programming because Beck (1999) sees it as the primary software development activity. In this spirit, Beck provides a complete and detailed description of the development techniques and related management practices that define XP.

XP is an attempt to focus on the activities that create real value for customers and avoid the bureaucracy that sometimes emerges from plan-driven processes. In this respect, XP is rather uncompromising, and its "dogmatism," as Meyer (2014, p. 139) calls it, has led to a notable polarization within the software development community. A large, loyal following of enthusiastic supporters has faced a large group of often fierce critics of the process. For example, claiming that its proponents have massively overhyped XP, Stephens and Rosenberg's (2003) book is a scathing and often sarcastic critique of it.

Of the agile processes, XP initially received the most attention in the years following the publication of the Agile Manifesto, and many organizations adopted it. At least in terms of adoption, it has more recently been overtaken by Scrum.

XP's popularity as a process may have waned lately, but many of the software development techniques that it popularized remain relevant and are now used together with Scrum, as Meyer (2014, p. 137) observes. For this reason, the method receives considerable, ongoing support from many experts who stress the importance of technical excellence in agile software development. One of them, Robert Martin (2020, p. 32), who too is an author of the Agile Manifesto, notes: "XP is the prototype, and the best representative, of the essential core of Agile."

The first edition of Beck's (1999) book on Extreme Programming defined the method and was a thought-provoking presentation, discussion, and synthesis of diverse ideas. It was published at a time when plan-driven processes were still dominant, and it drew much praise as well as criticism. Beck published a second edition in the year 2004, but it did not add fundamentally new ideas, as Meyer (2014, pp. 137) notes. Throughout this book, we will only refer to the version of XP defined in the first edition of Beck's book because it was current when the Agile Manifesto was published.

Scrum

Scrum is an agile process framework that Jeff Sutherland and Ken Schwaber developed in the 1990s, while Mike Beedle was an early adopter who helped refine it. All three are authors of the Agile Manifesto.

Unlike the UP and XP, which include technical practices specific to software development in the process definition, Scrum only provides a management and control process framework. It does not include techniques but can by design integrate practices that organizations already use or that are part of software processes like XP (Schwaber & Beedle 2001, p. 2).

Like the UP, Scrum targets a wide range of project sizes and types, and there are two ways to tailor the process. First, the freedom to choose the technical practices used with the Scrum process allows a certain degree of tailoring. Second, while an individual Scrum team should have less than ten members, it is possible to scale up the process by arranging "scrum of scrums" meetings that coordinate the work of multiple teams (Larman 2003, pp. 110).

Meyer (2014, pp. 139) notes that Scrum has become the leading agile process used for software development in organizations. It may seem like an unlikely success story, given that it does not include specific software development practices. On the other hand, the lack of technical detail avoids the kind of controversy that has affected XP, Scrum's closest competitor, and the ability to accommodate a wide range of technical practices certainly adds to its appeal. Another notable success factor that Meyer highlights is a very effective marketing operation.

Since Schwaber and Beedle's (2001) seminal book on Scrum, published in the same year as the Agile Manifesto, the process has attracted much interest and gone through an evolution. Although the book does not reflect this evolution, it is still a fair representation of Scrum and its theoretical background. It is the version of Scrum we refer to in this book.

Authority Structure

Royce (1998) describes the approach to software project management that is typically associated with plan-driven processes. It reflects his view that "[p]roject management is not a spectator sport" (p. 160). What he describes are project managers who actively manage teams, their work, and how they work. The approach rests on the assumption that the teams will not question the dominant role of project managers.

The Agile Manifesto questions the need for dominant project managers. It promotes the use of self-organizing teams, which plan and organize much of their work themselves. They do not have a role like the powerful, hands-on manager that Royce describes. Instead, agile software processes move many of the role's responsibilities to other team members.

XP teams provide a good illustration of how the redistribution of responsibilities looks in practice. The three essential roles in them are programmer, customer representative, and team coach. Each of them includes some of the activities that Royce assigns to project managers.

There is still a need for a management role in this scenario, which Beck (1999, p. 147) jokingly calls "big boss." In principle, it is the same role that Royce describes but without the responsibility for planning and organizing the work of teams on a daily basis. These XP project managers remain influential because they retain the right to intervene whenever necessary, but they should interfere as little as possible. They also remain responsible for high-level management activities like budgeting, staffing, and controlling, which gives them considerable leverage over teams.

The main stakeholders in an XP project are the programmers, the team coach, the customer representative, and the project manager. They share power and need to work together to achieve successful project outcomes. To this end,

XP acts as a framework that distributes the rights and duties of the project stakeholders with the aim to establish a productive balance of power that encourages collaboration and self-organization.

Plan-driven and agile software processes distribute formal authority among project stakeholders in fundamentally different ways. It shows that a software process is not just a technical solution to the problem of work organization. It also represents the intention to give more power to some stakeholders and less to others. Because the distribution of power in organizations tends to be controversial, it follows that the choice of software process in an organization is also a political decision.

While software processes substantially influence the distribution of power in projects and organizations, their creators and proponents rarely recognize this function. They usually prefer to justify the authority structures established by software processes with apolitical, rational, and technical arguments, while they treat the intended distribution of power as a minor side effect of technical necessity that does not warrant attention.

The reluctance to look into power-related aspects of software processes obscures the fact that their specific ways to distribute power between stakeholders are, of course, not solely the result of rational and technical necessity. Instead, like other aspects of organizational structure, software processes are usually selected and put in place by people in power, and it can be expected that their power interests guide their choice to a considerable degree.

It can safely be assumed that, in virtually all organizations, the people who ultimately make the decision to introduce a new software process are senior managers. Therefore, not least for marketing reasons, the creators and proponents of software processes need to emphasize features that sound appealing to senior managers.

The Agile Manifesto could be misunderstood as a challenge to the power of management in organizations because it calls for the use of self-organizing teams and minimal direct intervention by managers. It is not the case, and its purpose is to promote a purportedly better way to develop software, which is entirely consistent with the management priority of productivity. The manifesto does not challenge management but mismanagement in the form of overly bureaucratic processes. Consequently, as Meyer (2014, p. 57) clarifies, agile methods like XP and Scrum do not question managerial prerogative and fully subscribe to the priority of productivity.

Software processes are ultimately instruments for the control of software development by management. A crucial difference lies in how they try to accomplish it. While plan-driven processes try to concentrate power in the hands of project managers, agile processes try to establish a balance of power between multiple stakeholders.

Informal Power

Royce (1998) ignores the relationship between software processes and power. Without much explanation, he takes the idea for granted that the best way to run projects is to put project managers in charge and concentrate power in their hands at the expense of other stakeholders. The possibility that a software process that openly privileges managers and makes success largely dependent on their skills might face resistance from developers or other stakeholders seems to play no role in Royce's thinking.

The view that the design of an organization's authority structure can largely determine its internal power distribution is widely held among managers. It is to a certain degree correct, but it is necessary to keep in mind that there are limits to the effectiveness of formal authority in organizations because there are also other bases of power.

A typical situation in software development where the limits of formal authority become visible is when developers resist a software process imposed by management. Management-centric, bureaucratic processes of the type DeMarco and Lister (2013, p. 177) call a "Big M Methodology" have frequently been the target of resistance from developers.

One reason for excessively bureaucratic software processes is the difficulty to tailor large and complex frameworks like the UP to a project. Where the required specialist knowledge is not available, tailoring sometimes does not happen at all, but even where it happens, it may be performed by dedicated process engineers without much involvement of developers. If the resulting software processes turn out to be inadequate for practical use, it inevitably requires specialist knowledge, again, to adjust them through further tailoring. Additional tailoring causes costs, delays, and other problems, which may convince managers to keep the processes unchanged to save money and avoid risks.

When software developers are forced to work with unsuitable processes and have no practical, official way to change them, they sometimes get frustrated and resist. DeMarco and Lister (2013, p. 179) describe a form of resistance that is known as "malicious compliance" or "work to rule." It consists of purposefully taking the methodology too seriously by always following its prescriptions to the letter, especially where it is pointless and slows down the work. As a silent form of protest, it causes reduced productivity, which is, of course, the exact opposite of what the methodology promises.

Resistance through malicious compliance is, of course, political behavior. It severely challenges management because it targets productivity. Royce's ideas about software project management certainly have vast potential to cause this type of political behavior. Nevertheless, he pays no attention to it, and it is fair to say that organizational politics is a blind spot in his presentation.

Beck (1999), on the other hand, is keenly aware of the risk that software professionals and other stakeholders may resist a software process that does not sufficiently reflect their interests. Acknowledging that stakeholders in software projects may have different, competing goals, with XP, he attempts to mitigate the risk by design. The process needs to achieve a productive balance of power between the project stakeholders that encourages them to reconcile their differences constructively. It is the key to self-organizing teams, and the question is how to achieve it in practice.

Every XP team includes a coach who helps the team adopt the software process and learn to self-organize. According to Beck (1999, pp. 145), coaches need to understand XP in detail and have good people skills. Ideally, they have profound professional experience as programmers and do the same work as other team members but accept the additional responsibilities that come with the coach role. Assuming that the coaching process succeeds, Beck states that the role of a coach should become less relevant as the team matures. Consequently, an XP coach should withdraw to the degree to which a team displays self-organizing behavior.

How Beck describes the work of coaches in XP leaves no doubt that the role is primarily of an advisory nature. Coaches should point out observations, voice concerns, and make suggestions, and in this way, they can indirectly influence their teams, but they do not have the formal authority to overrule them. Ultimately, the team members decide how they take feedback and advice from their coaches into account. The coach role in XP is not meant to be particularly powerful, and coaches should certainly not dominate teams.

The reality of coaching in agile software development has sometimes been very different. Agile coach has become a recognized, prestigious job title in its own right, and the software process industry heavily promotes it as a valuable step on the career ladder. The prestige of the job title naturally attracts ambitious individuals, and the fact that there is only one coach on a team but many programmers underscores the special status of the role.

Especially the Scrum master role is at risk of exploitation by ambitious individuals who do not respect its limitations. Already the word "master" in its name likely sounds attractive to them, but another attraction is certainly that Schwaber and Beedle (2001, p. 31) define it as a management role. Moreover, Schwaber and Beedle present several anecdotes that highlight the role and depict Scrum masters as strong leaders who guide their rather clueless teams to success.

In light of the heroic image of Scrum masters that some authors project, it is not surprising that Ripley and Miller (2020) identify the "Superhero Scrum Master" (p. 80) and "Dreaded Scrum Lord" (p. 87) as major problems. To avoid such abuses of power, Scrum masters should ask themselves whether their actions serve their teams or their own agenda, Ripley and Miller advise. In the latter case, of course, Scrum masters engage in political behavior.

Martin (2020) shares the concern that agile coaches can become more powerful than the formal role implies and dominate teams. If it happens, he observes, coaches violate a core principle of agile software development because they impede team self-organization. In response, he presents a long list of things that an agile coach should not try to be (p. 143):

> The coach is not a manager. The coach is not responsible for budget or schedule. The coach does not direct the team nor does she represent the team's interests to management. The coach is not the liaison between the customers and the developers.

Agile coaches are arguably not supposed to carry out any of the activities that Martin lists, but if they ignore the limitations of the role, they are frequently able to generate substantial informal power. Martin tries to limit it by banning coaches from certain activities that are the responsibility of either project managers or teams. To this end, he also makes the pragmatic suggestion to rotate the coach role among team members on an informal schedule.

Regardless of the software process, stakeholders can achieve levels of power that are significantly different from their formal authority, and naturally, some try. It implies that the power distribution a process needs to work as intended cannot be taken for granted. Control is necessary to ensure that all stakeholders play by the rules.

Organizational Control

Even a well-designed software process offers no guarantee that all stakeholders will fully support it. There is always a substantial risk that some stakeholders will engage in activities that undermine the process to further their goals. Therefore, control is necessary to ensure that the process operates as intended.

For the illustration of certain key concepts of organizational control, Rollinson (2008, pp. 568) refers to the cybernetic model of control. This simple, well-known, universal model has been used in engineering, the natural sciences, the social sciences, and other disciplines to analyze and explain adaptive control in systems.

The fundamental idea behind cybernetic control is to regulate a transformation process through a feedback loop. The loop measures the actual outputs of the process and compares them to the desired outputs. If there is a deviation, the feedback mechanism adjusts the inputs to reduce it.

The application of the cybernetic model to software development is straightforward, and Schwaber and Beedle (2001, pp. 100) use the model to explain how empirical control works in Scrum. The process they choose to analyze is a sprint of 30 days. The main inputs of the process are the requirements, the technologies and the team, and the main output is the product increment at the end of the sprint. In the following, we shortly summarize some of Schwaber and Beedle's observations on the function of empirical control in Scrum.

The cybernetic model of control identifies three fundamental ways how the management of an organization can exert control over the process:

- Input control
- Output control
- Process control

Input control is most important for the first sprint when managers can select the initial inputs of the software process. The choice of requirements, technologies, and team members significantly influences how well a project starts. At the start of a project, input control gives managers a way to control the outputs of the process through its inputs. Because no outputs are available at this stage, managers have to base their selection of inputs on assumptions about the process. The assumptions can be unreliable, especially if there is little experience with the process, which can severely limit the applicability of input control.

Output control occurs at the end of every sprint in the form of the sprint review. It is usually preferred over input control because it depends on actual outputs, which reduces the need for potentially unreliable assumptions. During the sprint review, the stakeholders inspect the functional, tested product increment, which constitutes the main output of the process. Based on the evaluation of the product increment, management can decide to take corrective action and change the team, provide training, or make other adjustments to the inputs of the process.

Adjustments to inputs only affect the following sprint. It means that there can be a delay of up to 30 days before corrective action takes effect. Corrective action is only reliable to the degree that managers understand how the process works because they need to predict what changes they have to make to achieve the desired effects on the outputs.

Process control is the ongoing control activity that takes place during a sprint. Arguably, its most visible sign is the daily Scrum meeting, which allows the Scrum team to plan and coordinate its work for the following 24 hours. Process control during a sprint is primarily the responsibility of the Scrum team. To this end, a sprint is a time-boxed effort that allows the team to figure out how to achieve the sprint goal. Managers should minimize interventions during sprints because they usually impair the process of team self-organization.

Any practical software process depends on input control to manage software projects, and usually, the most critical aspect is team selection by managers. Its importance has been highlighted for decades by countless experts, for example, DeMarco and Lister (1987, 2013). The Agile Manifesto offers similar advice, and one of its principles states it very clearly: "Build projects around motivated individuals. Give them the environment and support they need, and trust them to get the job done."

Input control in the form of team selection is, without a doubt, a very desirable form of control in software projects. There is plenty of credible evidence confirming its benefits. On its own, though, it is usually not sufficient for the success of projects, as Meyer (2014, pp. 55) rightly cautions. Because their resources are limited and software development is not a priority in many, organizations routinely try to save money by hiring less qualified individuals. It can, overall, be the most cost-effective approach to staffing, but one consequence is that software developers are often not experienced, talented, or motivated enough to achieve maximum productivity without ongoing managerial oversight and direction.

Because input control is usually not sufficient for successful software development, all practical software processes integrate output control. It plays a central role in iterative software development processes because each iteration represents a complete control cycle. Output control can be very effective, but it suffers from two serious drawbacks. The first is the delay before a problem is addressed, which can be long and waste resources. Iterative processes try to reduce delays with short iterations, but there are practical limits. The second is that managers need to adjust the inputs based on the outputs, which they can only do if they understand how the process works.

Input and output control on their own are so limited that they do not provide organizations with a sufficient guarantee of productive work. To further reduce the risk, software processes also involve process control. Process control in organizations aims at controlling what actually happens in work processes. Where humans execute a work process, it essentially equates to behavioral control.

Process control takes place while the process operates. It is a continuous management activity, unlike input or output control, which only occur periodically. For this reason, process control is a relatively noticeable form of control, and as far as behavioral control is concerned, it aims to make sure that individuals do their work and do it right.

Because they have different perspectives and priorities, managers and developers may not always agree on the best approach to software development. Managers use behavioral control to ensure that developers do not simply do whatever they want in these cases. They have every reason to be concerned, as some advice for developers offered by Mancuso (2014) demonstrates. Mancuso raises the question of how to convince a manager of a new technical practice. His answer may alarm managers (p. 196): "The simple answer is you don't. It's easier to ask for forgiveness than to get permission. Just go there and do it."

One reason for Mancuso's advice is his belief that managers should trust qualified developers to do their job right. Whether the highly political behavior that he suggests helps build trust with managers can be doubted. It certainly has the potential to cause distrust, but in any case, most managers know that subordinates sometimes hide things from them. To mitigate the risk, managers usually attempt to balance trust and control. Because humans almost universally dislike the thought of being controlled by another person, as Rollinson (2008, p. 586) observes, developers may not like it. It shows that control is a touchy subject in organizations and indicates the challenge for management to implement it without much resentment.

Bureaucratic Control

Some form of control in organizations is necessary to ensure that subordinates do what their managers want, which cannot be taken for granted. In a bureaucracy, most of the necessary control occurs indirectly through rules and other elements of organizational structure. Work processes are highly standardized, and managers only intervene in exceptional circumstances. In this chapter, we look at how bureaucratic control works in software processes.

Bureaucracy

Standardization of organizational activities means that they are always carried out in the same way and to the same standards. The primary goal is to minimize unplanned variations in work processes and outputs. Because it helps avoid problems caused by the faulty execution of work, standardization minimizes the need for intervention by managers. It reduces costs because it makes activities very efficient but also has many other advantages. In particular, standardized work processes facilitate planning, their outputs are highly predictable, and systematic process improvement is straightforward.

© Peter Wendorff 2022
P. Wendorff, *Politics in Software Development*,
https://doi.org/10.1007/978-1-4842-7380-7_6

Standardization is the core idea behind a type of organizational structure generally known as "bureaucracy." In the minds of many people, bureaucracy has a negative reputation. It invokes images of managers and public servants who senselessly follow arcane rules and procedures that at first glance do not make any sense at all in the given situation. While this experience is not uncommon, it is also true that appropriate bureaucracy is beneficial and helps make public as well as private organizations highly efficient and equitable.

Bureaucracy plays a central role in software development, although it is rarely acknowledged. All software processes use bureaucratic principles to a greater or lesser extent. Based on the specific requirements of software development, they offer prescriptions that attempt to standardize development activities.

Because plan-driven software processes focus on planning and predictability, they tend to be bureaucratic. The UP is a case in question and standardizes software development to a very high degree of detail. Naturally, the generic process framework provides a degree of detail that is unnecessary for most projects, and the common failure to scale it down sufficiently has created an impression of excessive bureaucracy. Agile processes are a direct response to this perception and are not least an attempt to avoid unproductive bureaucracy.

Bureaucracy is a comprehensive set of ideas about the best way to structure organizations. Control is a central aspect of it, which applies to inputs, outputs, and processes. All three forms of control play an important role in bureaucratic organizations, but for their members, the most visible part is usually process control because it directly targets their behavior.

The control of human activities in bureaucratic organizations strongly relies on organizational structure. It minimizes the discretion of those who work in organizations and prescribes how they must carry out their work. Some of the defining characteristics of bureaucracy pertinent to control are (Fulop et al. 2009, p. 207; Rollinson 2008, pp. 532):

- There is a hierarchy with an explicit chain of command
- Work is planned, organized, and supervised by dedicated managers, who are accountable for results
- Activities of individuals are regulated by precisely defined, rational policies, rules and procedures that prescribe in detail how to carry out tasks and how work is coordinated
- Division of labor is achieved through precisely defined roles with clearly assigned responsibilities and tasks
- All relevant activities are recorded

Bureaucratic control is the aspect of bureaucracy concerned with controlling human behavior in organizations through organizational structure. It replaces direct control by managers with indirect control through hierarchies, roles, policies, rules, procedures, and other structural means that standardize activities. While bureaucracy relies on bureaucratic control where possible, managers still play a vital role in it for three reasons: They maintain the organizational structure, ensure that all members obey it, and deal with exceptions.

Managers are conspicuous representatives of formal authority in organizations. By reducing the need for direct managerial interventions, bureaucratic control depersonalizes control in organizations, making control less obtrusive. It has the advantage that it usually reduces resistance to control. At the same time, control becomes more efficient because managers spend less time on direct supervision.

The German academic Max Weber carried out the first systematic, comprehensive study of bureaucracy in organizations at the start of the 20th century. His work was groundbreaking and has been very influential ever since. Two central questions guiding Weber's investigation were why organizations become bureaucratic and what makes their members accept it (Fulop et al. 2009, pp. 204).

Weber's explanation for the tendency of many organizations to become bureaucratic is that in its ideal form, bureaucracy is not just any formal system, but one that embodies what he called "rational-legal authority." It is rational in the sense that it represents the systematic application of scientific, technological, and administrative knowledge, making work processes highly effective and efficient. It is legal in the sense that the application of the formal system always follows correct procedure, which reduces the scope for discrimination, favoritism, and other forms of political behavior. Where practical bureaucracy in organizations comes close to this ideal, it has clear advantages over informal approaches. Given these benefits, Weber expected that rational individuals generally support an adequate level of bureaucracy (Fulop et al. 2009, pp. 205).

In practice, bureaucracy establishes a mechanistic work environment that demands discipline and obedience. The norm is to follow the rules, and in extreme cases, humans virtually become a part of an efficient machine with very little influence in the workplace.

While the machine metaphor has always been attractive to the designers of organizations, the approach usually produces unwanted side effects, as Morgan (2006, pp. 28) points out. Among them are detrimental effects on the people working in bureaucratic organizations, in particular those at the bottom of the hierarchy. Mechanistically structured work can make them feel dehumanized, disempowered, and unappreciated. Often it results in resignation and mindless conformity, which inevitably harm productivity.

Another problem typical of bureaucracy is known as means-end-inversion. If it is difficult to measure the productivity of a bureaucratic process with certainty, it creates uncertainty about goal achievement. It frequently causes fear of failure, and the response of those in charge is often to slavishly follow the process to the letter, not least to avoid blame if anything goes wrong. The process is no longer just a means to an end, as it should be, and instead becomes an end in itself (Rollinson 2008, p. 486).

DeMarco and Lister (2013) give an example of means-end-inversion in the context of software processes. They make clear that development methodologies should be solely a means to an end, but note that they sometimes mutate into what they call a "Big M Methodology" (p. 177). The latter is a process that the stakeholders uncritically accept with blind faith and senselessly follow to the letter. It is no longer just a means to an end and instead becomes something important in its own right.

Managers

Bureaucratic control in organizations reduces the need for expensive personal control by managers. It achieves the reduction through standardized work processes, which usually make costly direct supervision less necessary. Provided individuals can be trusted to follow the system that managers have defined for the execution of their work, bureaucratic control is an attractive option to cut costs. In practice, it is often a very productive solution for predictable and well-understood work processes.

The possibility to standardize complex, knowledge-intensive work like software development is limited because it is usually impossible to make all necessary decisions based on rules, procedures, and other bureaucratic means. There will always be cases where a competent, authorized person will have to intervene to judge novel situations and make decisions. Software development is a typical example of an activity where unforeseen problems are the norm. A software process alone will often not give a clear answer, requiring human judgement. As a result, project managers still play a central role in the bureaucratic control of software processes.

While Jacobson et al. (1999) offer a very detailed description of the bureaucratic structure of the UP, Royce (1998) comprehensively covers corresponding management practices. Royce sees the management of software projects as a task that should be performed by dedicated project managers with considerable formal authority who effectively make all critical decisions and have substantial control over their development teams. While he offers some advice to managers on team building, he ignores the typical side effects of bureaucratic work organization on subordinates.

Royce suggests that managers should have certain "leadership qualities" (p. 45) to lead their teams successfully. However, the qualities he mentions mainly refer to ordinary management skills that have little to do with leadership. Royce describes a scenario where managers closely supervise teams that follow a detailed process and have very little discretion. His vision of management is entirely consistent with the principles of bureaucratic control. Where their intervention is necessary, managers rely on their formal authority and give instructions, which is the reason why this type of supervision is sometimes, usually in a pejorative sense, called "command-and-control" management.

Many managers in organizations practice the bureaucratic management style that Royce describes, and it sometimes works very well, but research on its effectiveness has identified some typical problems. One is that managers who try to practice close, hands-on control of a team often find it hard to cope with the amount of work it causes and can turn into bottlenecks. Another problem is that many subordinates regard tight supervision as unnecessary micromanagement, which can cause them to feel undervalued, lose motivation, become dependent, and disengage.

Automation

Already Max Weber recognized the documentation of activities as a fundamental principle of bureaucracy and an essential prerequisite of bureaucratic control. Record-keeping on paper in Weber's time required costly manual work and was of limited benefit because it was hard to share the information, which naturally restricted the practice. Process automation through information technology eliminates this restriction.

Because bureaucracy standardizes work processes, it creates ideal conditions for process automation. Jacobson et al. (1999, pp. 28) developed the UP to exploit this potential and designed it with tool support in mind. They regard software process automation as the most promising way to increase software development productivity in organizations.

Tool support does not only make work less onerous. When humans interact with a computer, the system can record their activities without additional cost. To the extent that they are automated, the data documents human activity in software processes. The collection of process data also enables the automatic verification of actions, and to some degree, the system can identify and block violations. It allows very effective bureaucratic control at a minimal cost.

Automatically recorded process data can also help managers address the timeless problem of status information in software development. Based on his extensive experience as a software project manager, Brooks (1995, pp. 156) notes that the first impulse of subordinates who fall behind schedule often is to hide the problem from their superiors. Possible reasons are fear of negative feedback or the hope that it will be possible to catch up later.

In many situations, this behavior is harmless and appropriate, and Brooks concludes that managers should expect it and not overreact, but he also recognizes their need to know if severe problems develop. He suggests two measures to solve the conflict: First, managers should avoid behavior that subordinates might perceive as threatening. Second, they should put safeguards in place to ensure that they always have access to the information they need, regardless of whether subordinates cooperate.

Software process automation offers a straightforward way to address both of Brooks' suggestions. In a fully automated process, comprehensive status data collection is a continuous process that invisibly operates in the background. Once the data is collected, it can be analyzed whenever necessary. Ideally, the information offers a current, accurate picture of work progress and allows to identify the reasons for any deviation from the plan. Subordinates are unlikely to feel threatened by the data collection process because automation makes it largely invisible, and they may not even be aware that they are under observation.

Automation enables tight bureaucratic control of software processes at a minimal cost, which managers undoubtedly find appealing, but it is not without problems. What Jacobson et al. (1999) ultimately suggest is the extensive use of computers instead of supervisors to control the work of software professionals. There can be no question that it inevitably amplifies the already problematic effects of bureaucratic organization on humans. The likely result is reduced productivity, which is the opposite of what Jacobson et al. promise.

Another problem can arise when individuals notice automatic status data collection and suspect it to play a role in performance appraisals. It is not difficult to imagine that some will try to game the system and engage in activities that primarily serve the purpose of generating good performance scores. Doing good work may become less attractive than creating the appearance of it. If it happens, the control system has the unintended side effect of incentivizing unproductive activities.

Alternatives

Bureaucratic control is a very cost-effective way for managers to control the behavior of subordinates. While it has limitations and often produces unwanted side effects, it is generally very effective and efficient if applied adequately. Its proven advantages explain why organizations that reach a size where mere command-and-control supervision is no longer enough usually become more bureaucratic. For the same reason, it plays a role in software processes and is the preferred control mechanism in plan-driven approaches like the UP.

The biggest problem with bureaucratic control is that it usually results in a mechanistic work environment that many humans dislike and find boring, which inevitably lowers their productivity. From a managerial point of view, it is a severe problem because the ultimate priority of management in most organizations is productivity.

Because of the well-known problems with bureaucratic control, organizations have always experimented with various alternative approaches. In many cases, they were attempts to better engage employees by giving them more say in the practical organization of their work. The initiatives were often successful and resulted in higher work motivation and job satisfaction. A closely related observation was that group-based work often delivered better results than individualized work.

In the 1970s, management experts increasingly came to the conclusion that organizations could be made more efficient by reducing management overheads and devolving some authority down the organizational hierarchy. The primary tool used to implement the shift of authority were self-managing teams, which typically have significant discretion to plan, organize, and control their work without direct managerial intervention (Rollinson 2008, pp. 342).

Self-managing teams require a significant relaxation of bureaucratic control. For managers, the crucial question is how to fill the void because organizational control is indispensable. From a theoretical point of view, the answer lies in the dimensions of power debate described in Chapter 2. Bureaucracy depends on the first two dimensions. When managers give instructions, they use the first, and bureaucratic control represents the second. The third dimension does not play a significant role in bureaucracy, but it is fundamental to self-managing teams, as we will see in Chapter 7.

Cultural Control

Bureaucratic control has many advantages and is proven to work in practice but also has many problems. One is that it only creates conformity, where people do their job but do not care much about it. Naturally, managers prefer if subordinates care about their work and try to do their best. The question is how to foster commitment to organizational goals like high productivity in members of organizations. The answer that has emerged is cultural control. In this chapter, we describe its main elements and explain its role in software development processes.

Self-Organizing Teams

Work teams are groups of people who collaborate to achieve shared goals. If a team member performs poorly, it affects the ability of the entire team to achieve its goals, and in this sense, teamwork makes members interdependent.

While some teams benefit from close supervision by a hands-on manager, not all do. Mature teams can often organize some aspects of their work themselves and become more productive if they have more discretion over their work. While management experts had observed this effect before, it was only in the 1970s when the idea gained ground that self-organized teamwork is an option to make organizations more productive.

DeMarco and Lister (1987) were notable early advocates of team self-organization in software development. Already in the first edition of their iconic book *Peopleware*, published in the late 1980s, they use the term "jelled

P. Wendorff, *Politics in Software Development*,
https://doi.org/10.1007/978-1-4842-7380-7_7

team" (p. 123) to denote a highly cohesive group of individuals who mainly organize their work themselves and require almost no attention from managers. DeMarco and Lister's key observation is that jelled teams can be exceptionally productive. Interest in the idea continued to grow for over a decade before the Agile Manifesto boosted it by endorsing self-organizing teams in one of its principles.

The terms "self-organizing" and "self-managing" team essentially mean the same. Both are widely used in the management literature, but because the authors of the manifesto chose the former, it is the preferred term in this book as well.

When the Agile Manifesto was published, team self-organization in software development marked a clear departure from the traditional hands-on project manager role that concentrates power in a single person. The idea fell on fertile ground because many software developers and other stakeholders were frustrated by projects that traditional project managers had mismanaged, often creating a frustrating and stressful work environment. In this climate, agile software development offered self-organization as a plausible alternative, and Meyer (2014, p. 53) is without a doubt right that it was one of the manifesto's main attractions.

If teams in an organization are given the right to self-organize to some degree, there is, of course, no guarantee that they will function as hoped and work toward the organizational goals. Therefore, managers carefully create the environment in which self-organization is allowed to take place. Schwaber and Beedle (2001, p. 2) metaphorically describe the approach as the creation of "incubators" that provide the conditions teams need to self-organize in the way managers want.

Typical measures that managers use to influence the self-organization of teams include (Schwaber & Beedle, p. 108; Cohn 2009, pp. 221):

- Creating or dissolving teams
- Adding or removing members
- Making resources available
- Giving more or less responsibility
- Rewarding group performance
- Changing the physical space
- Encouraging communication
- Asking hard questions
- Allowing sensible risk-taking

- Building tolerance for honest mistakes
- Encouraging dissenting viewpoints

While the list is far from complete, it indicates that the actions of managers influence the self-organization process indirectly. Managers do not directly tell them what to do, but their actions indirectly constrain what teams and individuals can do. The goal is to ensure that teams go in the right direction without burdening them with too many constraints. The approach is often called "subtle control" by its proponents. Cohn (2009, pp. 220) warns that it is a delicate balancing act because overly constrained teams usually become dependent on their managers and less likely to self-organize.

Most items in the list fall into two broad categories: resources and behavioral norms. Managers keep resources under control, which includes people, office space, tools, and money. In particular, they determine the composition of teams and how the members differ in terms of personality, qualification, knowledge, experience, and status. They also set the tone of the interactions between the team members by establishing some basic behavioral norms.

Even though managers of self-organizing teams try to avoid direct interference, they usually have the authority to intervene if necessary, particularly if teams underperform, misbehave, or cause other serious problems. Accordingly, members of self-organizing teams report to line or project managers.

In theory, team self-organization is an attractive proposition because it promises higher performance at a reduced cost for supervision by managers, but research shows that it is also hard to achieve in practice. For self-organization to be advantageous, facilitating factors need to be in place. One is a reward system that incentivizes team rather than individual performance. Another is a robust conflict resolution mechanism. In general, making self-organization work in practice is a challenge (Robbins & Judge 2019, pp. 359).

Managers of self-organizing teams stay in control of resources, and because they occasionally adjust them based on team performance, it constitutes input and output control. The behavioral norms they establish constitute process control, but often they seem like mere common sense, and one may wonder how they can be enough to keep teams under control. The concept of organizational culture offers an intriguing answer to this question.

Organizational Culture

The concept of culture plays a central role in disciplines like anthropology, sociology, and social psychology. Culture is something that groups of individuals share and that influences how they make sense of their environment. They may not always be aware of it, but to some extent, the members of a culture think, feel, and behave in similar ways. It is straightforward to apply the concept of culture to the members of organizations, and the idea became popular in the early 1980s, mainly under the label "organizational culture."

Countless authors have approached the subject of organizational culture from various angles. While these efforts have not resulted in a generally accepted definition of the concept, there is broad agreement that the behavior of an organization's members is to a considerable extent and largely invisibly guided by its culture. In essence, it tells individuals what behavior is acceptable and what is not. It is mainly this capacity to influence the behavior of individuals in organizations that makes organizational culture a core subject in management.

Probably, the best-known attempt to capture the essence of organizational culture is Edgar Schein's layered model. It consists of three interrelated levels of meaning that members of an organization share. The fundamental idea behind the model is that for members of the culture as well as outsiders, the levels are not equally discernible. They are (Rollinson 2008, pp. 592):

- Basic assumptions
- Values and beliefs
- Artifacts and creations

Basic assumptions form the least accessible of the three levels. They are deep beliefs that feel natural to the members of a culture and are so much taken for granted that they mainly operate at the subconscious level. For example, in an organization with a unitary culture, the members instinctively feel uncomfortable when they notice conflict, including openly competitive behavior. Conversely, in a pluralist culture, the members do not find civilized disagreement disturbing but rather stimulating, and they see competitive behavior as a natural part of the game.

The level of values and beliefs is informed by the level of basic assumptions but is more accessible. It provides the moral and rational justification of actions and is indirectly noticeable because it is relatively easy to observe actions. For example, in an organization with a unitary culture, the members strongly value win-win solutions. If they face disagreements, stakeholders are often willing to sacrifice some of their own ambitions for the sake of a fair settlement. Because they value openness, honesty, and collaboration, they regard political behavior as unnecessary and undesirable. The belief that there is no room for politics marks a fundamental difference to a pluralist culture, which highly values political skill and sees it as the ability to get things done in organizations.

The level of artifacts and creations represents directly noticeable manifestations of a culture. They result from actions representing the layer of values and beliefs. In the context of the culture to which they belong, the artifacts and creations have a deeper meaning that is usually not clear to outsiders. Although outsiders can directly perceive the manifestations, they struggle to make sense of the artifacts and creations unless an insider explains their hidden meaning. Six central areas where a culture manifests itself are:

- Norms
- Language
- Symbols
- Rites and ceremonies
- Myths and stories
- Taboos

The concept of culture does not only apply to organizations in their entirety but also parts. Branches, departments, and teams can develop subcultures, which may be significantly different from the surrounding organizational culture.

In software development, culture is frequently observed at the team level. When team members of well-functioning teams interact, over time, they tend to adjust to one another and focus on shared assumptions, values, and beliefs, rather than differences. Gradually, a basic, informal, implicit agreement about the right way to work together emerges. Where a strong culture develops, the members have reached a consensus about all critical aspects of their work as a team, which drastically reduces the chance of conflict and makes very high performance possible.

Well-functioning XP teams develop a culture that values the courage to face reality. Their members know that when it comes to technical solutions, wishful thinking is not enough, and they are not afraid to put it to the test despite the possibility of disappointment. Because XP requires teams to show courage, Beck (1999, pp. 33) includes it in the form of a value in the definition of XP. As courage is a part of the software process, it is the responsibility of coaches to ensure that the behavior of teams reflects appropriate courage.

The value plays a central role in an anecdote presented by Beck (1999, p. 74), and we use it to demonstrate how Schein's model helps make sense of cultural phenomena. It is an example of how a value can give rise to a symbol that in turn supports the value, illustrating what the levels in Schein's model represent and how they interact.

As Beck recounts, the story started with his observation that design meetings of an XP team that he coached took hours to finish and did not even deliver usable solutions. Realizing that these meetings were often too long and a waste of time, he concluded that the participants sometimes preferred talking to coding. His explanation for the behavior was fear that executable code might have revealed problems with proposed solutions. Assuming the behavior was the result of fear, Beck wanted to remind the team that the courage to face reality is essential in XP. To this end, he bought an ordinary kitchen timer and placed it in a visible position in the meeting room. He then told the team about his observations and set a time limit of 10 minutes for design meetings.

According to Beck, the timer was maybe never used as a timing device. Nevertheless, because it had become a symbol of wasted time and a lack of courage, its visible presence was enough to have a profound effect on the behavior of the team members. It became a part of the team's culture, and for members, it had a special meaning that went far beyond its mere technical function. For outside observers, without knowledge of the culture, it would have been impossible to figure out what it symbolized to the team.

The symbolic meaning of the kitchen timer did not naturally emerge from the interactions of the team members. Instead, Beck acting as the team's coach, created the symbol to remind its members that courage is a value in XP, but the symbol worked indirectly. It appears unlikely that the word "courage" came to their mind each time team members saw the kitchen timer. However, when they saw it, stopped the meeting and created executable code to test their ideas, their actions showed courage and reinforced the value.

The culture of teams usually develops over a long time with no guarantees regarding the outcome. Beck's anecdote demonstrates the risk of an unsatisfactory culture because the team had developed one before he intervened. Part of the team culture was the belief that debating the merits of ideas was more desirable than acting to put them to the test. The risk inherent in the process suggests to guide culture development by defining a model culture that can serve as a template.

XP is an example of this approach. Beck (1999, p. 29) refers to a pivotal function of culture in human societies when he notes that they develop shared sets of values that mitigate conflicts caused by goal differences of their members. Realizing the potential of culture to manage conflict, Beck continues to define a set of four values for XP teams: communication, simplicity, feedback, and courage. He emphasizes that respect is another fundamental

XP value underlying the four. Beck leaves no doubt that for XP to work successfully, the values need to become a natural habit of the team members. Accordingly, XP includes several principles and practices that represent and reinforce the values.

The XP values are an attempt to control the culture of teams by providing the blueprint of a productive culture that is tailored to XP and supports it in the best possible way. Rather than wait for team culture to emerge naturally, the core idea is to accelerate and guide the process. Once the culture is in place, it invisibly controls the behavior of the team members and minimizes the need for other forms of control.

Cultural control is the management practice to control the behavior of individuals in organizations through culture. It fundamentally depends on the ability of managers to shape the culture of organizations. Systematic activities of managers aimed at building or changing organizational culture to align it better with organizational goals became popular among management experts in the 1980s under the label "cultural engineering."

Cultural Engineering

In software development, cultural engineering most frequently targets the team level. The goal is to shape the culture of teams so that their members do what their managers want them to do but without direct supervision. Teams where this approach succeeds take ownership of tasks set by managers, show extraordinary commitment to accomplish them, and take pride in high performance. They self-organize and require minimal managerial supervision because their members voluntarily comply with the demands of their managers.

Cultural engineering is a way to build self-organizing teams with a productive culture, which is the primary reason why managers take great interest in the subject. In particular, agile software processes that depend on self-organizing teams usually integrate a wide range of cultural engineering techniques, and Beck's (1999) XP is an obvious example of this practice.

Another example is Scrum. Schwaber and Beedle (2001) refer to organizational culture and related concepts in several places in their book. Although they do not explicitly refer to it, their observations align remarkably well with Schein's layered model. In particular, in chapter 9 of the book, Schwaber and Beedle define and explain a set of five Scrum values: commitment, focus, openness, respect, and courage. Scrum critically rests on the values, and team members must embrace them to make the process work successfully.

Schwaber and Beedle leave no doubt that cultural engineering is an essential part of Scrum. Already in the introduction to their book, they clearly state that "Scrum is a kind of social engineering" (p. 2). The reference to social engineering is highly relevant because it is very closely related to cultural engineering, and some commentators use the two terms interchangeably. In this book, we see the latter as a special case of the former. We regard cultural engineering as the application of social engineering techniques by managers targeting the culture of organizations.

A substantial section with the heading "Anthropological View of Scrum" in Schwaber and Beedle (2001) further highlights the relationship to organizational culture. The section starts with the claim that "practicing Scrum changes the culture of an organization" (p. 118). Shortly later, Schwaber and Beedle implicitly refer to the level of artifacts and creations in Schein's model when they note that "some Scrum practices can also be seen as ceremonies and rites, like the Scrum meetings or the Sprint planning meetings" (p. 119).

Schwaber and Beedle (2001, p. 119) conclude the section with short descriptions of some typical cultural engineering techniques. The list includes:

- Holding meetings at the same place at the same time and in the same way to turn them into ceremonies that help teams bond and jell

- Telling stories like the chickens and pigs fable to communicate core ideas in an interesting, humorous, or dramatic way

- Changing the language by introducing and enforcing the Scrum vocabulary because it helps change the culture

- Adding mentors who embody the Scrum culture and can act as role models to groups that need culture change

- Establishing group practices that constantly highlight, demonstrate, and reinforce the five Scrum values

- Providing presentations and documents to reinforce the belief that Scrum is different from alternative approaches and more likely to work

The list of techniques gives a good idea of how cultural engineering techniques work in practice. While they believe that managers can change organizational culture, Schwaber and Beedle (2001, p. 119) warn that it is one of the most complex management tasks.

Their warning is echoed by DeMarco and Lister (2013). Given their positive observations about jelled teams, it is no surprise that they initially planned to include a chapter in their book with concise, prescriptive advice for managers on how to build them. However, despite their best efforts, they found it impossible to write. Instead, they offer some pragmatic advice in part IV of their book. Interestingly, as the authors themselves note, their recommendations predominantly cover actions that managers should avoid because they stop teams from jelling. It indicates how difficult it is to give prescriptive advice on the subject.

To apply cultural engineering to teams, managers need to address two challenges that are central to the approach. The first is to define a culture that encourages the desired behavior and make the teams adopt it. The second is to create conditions where the teams become self-disciplining and use peer pressure to maintain and reinforce the culture.

To address the first challenge, managers usually define a set of team values, which are essentially abstract rules that characterize the behavior expected of team members. Typically, the values emphasize the importance of collaboration and define what it takes to be seen as a good team member, while they discourage individualism. To make them sound attractive and rewarding, values used for cultural engineering always have a positive connotation. Typical values in use for cultural engineering include, of course, the four XP values and the five Scrum values. Another suggestion comes from Fitzpatrick and Collins-Sussman (2015, pp. 11), who have successfully built productive teams using the three values humility, respect, and trust, which they call "principles."

The second challenge for managers is to create conditions in which teams maintain and reinforce their culture through peer pressure. Peer pressure only works if the team members can observe one another. Therefore, it is critical to make the activities of the team members transparent so that they can constantly monitor each other, identify those who deviate from the team culture, and put pressure on them to adjust their behavior.

While cultural engineering, in theory, allows to control the behavior of teams and make them productive, the practical results in organizations have been mixed for various reasons.

Beck's (1999, p. 156) experience with XP points to the existing culture as a frequent barrier to the successful adoption of XP in organizations. As he observes, conflict is inevitable if the culture of XP teams clashes with that of their environment. Generalizing Beck's observation, it appears likely that cultural engineering faces severe problems if the target culture is incompatible with the surrounding culture.

Another reason for poor results is individuals who are not malleable enough for successful cultural engineering. To avoid sanctions, they usually hide their true beliefs and feign commitment to an imposed team culture but secretly do not care about it and pursue their own interests regardless of the consequences. The problem is often made worse by the difficulty for managers to detect it (Rollinson 2008, pp. 585).

Cultural engineering can also run into trouble if managers see it as just another tool at their disposal to increase productivity and are not willing to change anything else, in particular, give up part of their power or change their behavior toward their subordinates. A culture of productive self-organization creates mutual obligations between managers and teams. Cultural engineering will only produce cynicism and disillusionment if managers fail to honor their part of the deal (Rollinson 2008, p. 344).

DeMarco and Lister's (1987, 2013) ideas on growing jelled teams are essentially a collection of simple cultural engineering dos and don'ts. As Schwaber and Beedle (2001) and Fitzpatrick and Collins-Sussman (2015) offer similar advice, it is fair to say that cultural engineering in software development has been advocated for over three decades now. The approach is certainly appealing and has potential, but there is no doubt that its implementation remains a challenge for managers.

Leadership

Personal control of individuals in organizations has been in use for centuries, and already the early writers on management, for example, Henri Fayol and Max Weber, described it in great detail and saw it as a central activity of managers. It means that two individuals are in direct contact while one exerts control over the behavior of the other. Another term in use in the management literature is "direct control." Personal control represents the first dimension of power and can rely on any of the bases of power described in Chapter 2.

Bureaucratic control establishes a simple, hierarchical authority structure where every subordinate is directly supervised by a superior. It thus lays the foundation for personal control based on formal authority. In software development, it is the type of management that Royce (1998) describes. It is characteristic of software processes like the UP that primarily rely on bureaucratic control. In essence, it means that powerful project managers ultimately make all critical decisions and have comprehensive control over their development teams. They may occasionally involve subordinates in the decision-making process, but there is no doubt about who has the last word.

The type of direct control that bureaucratic control implies is unsuitable if managers want to build self-organizing teams. Close supervision based on formal authority essentially means the opposite of giving teams substantial freedom to organize their work as they see fit. If subordinates are given more discretion over their work, an alternative to personal control based on formal authority is needed. The solution that has for decades been touted in the business literature is leadership.

Not least because the popular business press has sometimes exaggerated the role of leaders in anecdotal success stories, some managers prefer to think of themselves as leaders, as Rollinson (2008, p. 354) notes. Unsurprisingly, the tendency exists in software development too, and Fitzpatrick and Collins-Sussman (2015, p. 53) demonstrate it with their advice to avoid the term "manager" and use "leader" instead. It is questionable advice, though, because both terms have their place in management. While they are closely related, they denote different concepts, and mixing them up is not helpful.

It is easier to explain what a leader is if it is clear what a manager is and how the two roles differ. Rollinson (2008, pp. 354) provides definitions of both roles, which can be summarized as follows:

- Manager: An individual in an organization who is officially appointed to a position that includes the formal authority to control the behavior of subordinates to a certain extent

- Leader: An individual who satisfies certain desires and expectations of followers, who in return allow the leader to influence their behavior to a certain extent

The crucial difference between the two roles is that subordinates must comply with the legitimate demands of their managers, while followers do not have to comply with the demands of their leaders. In other words, managers can force compliance, while leaders cannot.

Leaders have to persuade their followers to comply, which may be difficult, but where they succeed, they can assume that compliance is voluntary, which reduces the need for other forms of control. Managers, on the other hand, do not have to convince their subordinates. Instead, they can take compliance for granted and even enforce it with disciplinary measures. For them, it is relatively easy to achieve compliance, but it may not be entirely voluntary, which increases the need for control.

Because manager and leader are roles, an individual can be in both at the same time. Depending on which of the two is more pronounced in a given situation, compliance may result from formal authority, the other bases of power or a combination of both. As noted above, if the goal is team self-organization, the first option is a mismatch, leaving only two relevant role combinations:

- Manager and leader
- Leader

Fitzpatrick and Collins-Sussman (2015) favor the first combination. In their view, every project needs a strong manager who is in command and ultimately responsible for its success. They advocate cultural engineering for team-building, which they regard as a critical success factor because leadership is only an option where teams are likely to follow. Otherwise, they note, managers need to play a more directive role. The leader behavior that Fitzpatrick and Collins-Sussman describe is, therefore, backed up by substantial formal authority, which allows a manager to force compliance when leadership fails or is not an option.

The second role combination is leadership alone, which is not backed up by corresponding formal authority. A clear example is the coach role in XP, which comes with minimal additional power. Nevertheless, if necessary, coaches are expected to develop significant influence over the behavior of teams. Without the formal authority needed to force compliance, their only option is leadership. XP coaches can only persuade teams of their ideas but not impose them.

Cultural engineering requires leadership. It can be provided by a manager with leadership skills, as Fitzpatrick and Collins-Sussman (2015) suggest, or by a leader without a management role, as Beck (1999) assumes.

Peer Pressure

Cultural control relies on peer pressure to maintain and reinforce the culture of teams. Peer pressure plays a fundamental role in the socialization processes in groups of individuals inside and outside of organizations. It takes place if an individual in a group engages in discretionary behavior to comply with group norms. The more willing the group members are to discipline deviant behavior, the more pressure there is to comply.

To increase the willingness of team members to put pressure on one another, managers often hold them collectively accountable for performance and outcomes. It creates an incentive for the members to put pressure on poorly performing peers to avoid collective failure.

Another way to make peer pressure more effective is to increase the legitimacy of teams in the eyes of their members. The more members respect their teams, the more willing they are to comply with their norms. Therefore, proponents of cultural control usually portray teams as entities with strong identities of their own and unquestionable moral authority. According to this rhetoric, teams exert impartial control to maintain discipline in the interest of all their members.

How peer pressure works in practice is exemplified by an anecdote that Cockburn (2001, p. 69) calls the "peer pressure ritual." According to Cockburn, Kent Beck used the ritual in the C3 project, which was the first large project that Beck (1999) used to develop and refine XP.

XP emphasizes the avoidance of over-engineered software designs, and simplicity is one of the method's four values. As Cockburn recalls, the C3 team did not always try hard enough to find simple solutions, resulting in unnecessary complexity, and Beck needed to remind its members of the value. To this end, Beck used the peer pressure ritual, which Cockburn (2001, p. 69) describes as follows:

> [T]he group formed a procession, placed a propeller beanie on the head of someone with an overly clever solution, and then spun the propeller on the beanie, commenting on the "cleverness" of the solution.

What Cockburn describes here is a rather overt application of peer pressure through playful, public shaming. The purpose of the ritual is not only its immediate effect on the offender. Instead, Cockburn observes, it also warns all team members that they must respect the value. In terms of Schein's layered model, the ritual is a visible manifestation of the culture, and whenever the team performs it, it reinforces the value.

Schwaber and Beedle (2001) are very open about their endorsement of peer pressure. For example, they observe (p. 153): "Nothing helps people do their best, despite their shortcomings, as much as group pressure and a team environment."

Unsurprisingly, Scrum includes several practices that exploit the effect of peer pressure. The timeless problem of managers that subordinates sometimes withhold or distort status information, which we described in Chapter 6, can serve as an example. Scrum addresses the issue by including openness in its five values. It means that everything has to be visible to everybody at any time. Scrum tries to remove the ability to hide anything, as Schwaber and Beedle (2001, p. 151) make clear.

An occasion where it is highly relevant that the participants observe the value is the daily Scrum meeting. It does not only serve the purpose of collecting status information about everybody's work progress. Instead, Schwaber and Beedle (2001, p. 105) explain, the meeting's formal structure also "makes everybody say it in front of everybody else." As they observe, promising in front of colleagues is also a matter of honor, which forces team members to be open and honest. The presence of their peers puts pressure on individuals not to lie or hide anything important. One consequence of the peer pressure at the meeting is that managers have a better chance to receive accurate status information.

The Scrum value openness has another crucial function. Peer pressure in teams can only develop if their members can easily observe everything their teammates do. By creating the required transparency, the value enables peer pressure. It demonstrates the symbiotic relationship between the value and peer pressure in Scrum. The value promotes the visibility required for peer pressure, and peer pressure, in turn, helps create visibility.

As agile software processes such as XP and Scrum heavily rely on cultural control, it is not surprising that their creators and proponents see peer pressure as a force for good. For example, Beck (1999) and Schwaber and Beedle (2001) emphatically promote its use for the achievement of organizational goals like discipline and productivity. While the Agile Manifesto does not mention peer pressure, its application has become a central pillar of agile thinking. A typical example is Adkins (2010, p. 119), an experienced agile coach, who concludes: "Healthy agile teams experience peer pressure."

While many authors readily recognize the benefits of peer pressure, they are less vocal about the potential problems it can create. For example, it is also likely to cause stress, tension, and conflict in teams, which can be counterproductive and harm the morale and well-being of individuals. Moreover, the question must be asked, who is most affected by the problems. An inconvenient part of the answer is that team members at the bottom of the pecking order are more likely to become the target of peer pressure than those at the top.

Although it is certainly not the aspect the authors want to highlight, an anecdote presented by Schwaber and Beedle (2001, pp. 152) reveals how unpleasant the experience on the receiving end of peer pressure can be. It describes the experience of an engineer called "Dave" on a project where the first author Ken Schwaber served as Scrum master.

Dave's team had committed to a sprint goal, and as a part of it, Dave had accepted responsibility for some critical work, only to discover that he did not have the skills to carry it out fast and well enough. Dave's inability to fulfill his commitments slowed down the team. As Schwaber and Beedle recount, the other team members first showed solidarity and helped Dave with his problem.

As Dave continued to fall behind, the other team members became increasingly unhappy about the delays he caused, and the initial solidarity turned into resentment. To avoid facing criticism, Dave started to come later and later to work. Commenting on the situation, Schwaber and Beedle (2001, p. 152) note that the team "had found in Dave a convenient, if undeserving, scapegoat."

The situation continued for several days without a resolution. Eventually, with support from the Scrum master, Dave was able to find a creative solution to his problem and finally met the expectations of his team. He and the team learned valuable lessons from their experience, and Schwaber and Beedle leave no doubt about their view that peer pressure played a very positive role in the episode, despite Dave's stressful experience. For them, it is a clear case where the ends justify the means.

Dave's case illustrates that the instrumentalization of peer pressure in Scrum can cause significant stress for individuals. There is no evidence in Schwaber and Beedle's account that Dave did anything wrong, apart from misjudging his ability to perform a task. It is unclear why he committed to the work that later got him into trouble and whether he was under pressure to take more risk than he wanted. What is clear is that the team held him accountable for the work and put considerable pressure on him to make progress.

The way Dave's teammates treated him suggests that he was relatively low in the team's pecking order and had failed to build a power base. His lack of power made him an easy target and undoubtedly contributed to his fate as a scapegoat for his team. It is hard to imagine that the team would have treated its most respected member in the same way.

Instrumentalizing peer pressure in the workplace, Scrum purposely encourages team members to put pressure on another to advance organizational goals. Even though Scrum creates the conditions for peer pressure, it still requires the willingness of the team members to act accordingly.

In general, cultural control is critically dependent on the willingness of the controlled individuals to cooperate in their own control by maintaining the culture through peer pressure. Its reliance on the culture's members makes it vulnerable because control quickly breaks down when enough of them withdraw their cooperation.

The recognition that cultural control is vulnerable is the main reason why agile software processes include dedicated roles like the Scrum master and the XP coach. Agile coaches are responsible for maintaining cultural control, which requires them to regulate peer pressure in agile teams and keep it at a productive level. In particular, they are safeguards that help prevent situations where peer pressure gets out of control and harms individuals.

Unobtrusive Control

Tight behavioral control in organizations by managers is usually quite unpopular with the controlled individuals. To reduce resentment to control, organization designers try to make it less noticeable to the individuals subjected to it. This goal has driven interest in cultural control, which tries to make control as unobtrusive as possible. In software development, agile processes like XP and Scrum are clear examples of this trend.

The creators of Scrum openly embrace cultural control, but it proves controversial. Quoting claims by Jeff Sutherland and Ken Schwaber that subtle control in Scrum relies on "peer pressure" and "control by love," and that the process can reveal the "tacit (unconscious) knowledge" of the team, Meyer notes (p. 54):

> Words somewhat scary if you have been told that your team is self-organizing and suddenly learn that you are in fact being "subtly" controlled through "tacit" and "unconscious" techniques. The part about love may be reassuring; or not.

Meyer's criticism reflects the common misunderstanding that self-organization and subtle control in Scrum and other agile approaches imply a low level of control. It is not the case, and Schwaber and Beedle (2001) make it unambiguously clear that Scrum serves the purpose to give managers in organizations complete control over the software process. There is a crucial difference, though, and that is what Meyer finds problematic and even calls "scary": Scrum is designed to make control less noticeable.

Control in agile software processes tends to be unobtrusive, and it can mislead observers into believing that they focus less on organizational control than other processes like the UP. It is one of the reasons why, as Meyer (2014, p. 54) rightly criticizes, there is some confusion in the literature on agile software development about the status of managers.

The confusion arises because processes like XP and Scrum largely depend on cultural control, which is unobtrusive. It can create the wrong impression that managers are not in control and that self-organizing teams can effectively do what they want, which is, of course, not true. Instead, when teams adopt a culture engineered by their managers, the members internalize control through a process of socialization that strongly relies on peer pressure. They learn to follow the cultural norms and to maintain and reinforce them by monitoring and disciplining each other.

A closely related factor is the focus on leadership in agile processes. They rely on roles like the XP coach and Scrum master, which require strong leadership. Unlike managers, leaders cannot just tell others what to do but have to persuade them. It avoids the feeling in followers that they are under the control of another person and have no say. Instead, followers are more likely to experience the influence of their leaders as productive collaboration.

Bureaucratic control still plays a role in agile software processes. There are still rules and procedures to follow, and staff and budgets are still under the control of powerful managers. However, these managers focus on the big picture and leave the actual work to self-organizing teams. Nevertheless, ultimately they are in charge because they can terminate projects that do not deliver value for money or are no longer needed.

While agile processes do not eliminate bureaucratic control, they reduce it significantly through thoughtful combination with cultural control. The result is a sophisticated control regime, which can irritate observers who are used to the simplicity of management in plan-driven processes. From a managerial point of view, one highly appealing advantage of the more sophisticated regime is that resistance to management control becomes less likely and more difficult.

There is no reason to believe that agile processes like XP and Scrum give managers less control than plan-driven processes like the UP. On the contrary, cultural control can be intense because every team member controls the others, making control ubiquitous. Despite its ubiquitous nature in agile processes, they may appear relatively free of control, not least because they cloak it in very appealing rhetoric about values, teamwork, and leadership.

Political Action

Politics at Work

Organizations are also places where stakeholders with diverse interests compete for attention and resources. Therefore, the effective use of power to achieve goals is critical to stakeholder success in organizations. Effective political action is a learnable skill, and numerous books on office politics indicate significant interest in it. Software professionals who turn to this kind of literature may be surprised to find that many things they have done or experienced in the workplace before are well-known forms of political behavior. In this chapter, we look at political skill and ethics.

Politics Is Pervasive

The first two parts of the book have shown that goal conflict in organizations is normal. Sometimes it stays latent, and at other times it develops into open conflict, where stakeholders use their power to resolve their differences through political processes. While there are large variations, it is safe to say that politics in the workplace is pervasive.

As a consequence, it is not surprising that many members of organizations believe, presumably based on their personal experiences, that politics matters for career progress. For example, Robbins and Judge (2019, p. 400) point to a poll that asked Americans about what matters for career progress in their organizations. 51% of the participants cited "politics," far ahead of "hard work" with 27% in second place.

P. Wendorff, *Politics in Software Development*,
https://doi.org/10.1007/978-1-4842-7380-7_8

Organizations assess the performance of their members, not least because their success depends on the identification and promotion of suitable candidates. Therefore, performance reviews take place in some form or shape in virtually all organizations, and because they can have serious consequences, they create competition among individuals who want to score well in them. But the promotion process is often not purely objective and rational, as Fitzpatrick and Collins-Sussman (2015, p. 114) observe. Superior work performance certainly plays a role in it, but they leave no doubt that systematic impression management and other political behavior can ultimately decide the "promotion game."

It is an inevitable part of organizational life that ambitious individuals compete with others for the same rewards, and often they use whatever power they have to get ahead of the competition. Even individuals who may have no intention to get involved in the political machinations of their organizations will still be affected by the activities of superiors, peers, or subordinates who engage in political behavior. It can be impossible to stay out of these activities if political players put pressure on others to support them.

Since the 1970s, there has been a shift from more hierarchical and bureaucratic structures to work in cross-functional teams in many organizations. The introduction of teamwork typically involved flatter organizational structures, fewer managers, and new roles. In software development, the shift toward teamwork became particularly visible with the publication of the Agile Manifesto in the year 2001.

Agile software processes, for example, XP and Scrum, depend on self-organizing teams. None of their members has much formal authority over the others, making the effective development and use of alternative power bases more relevant. Teams have considerable discretion over their work, not least to encourage creativity as well as the competition of different ideas. It makes organizations more flexible and responsive, but it also empowers individuals with diverse perspectives, stimulating conflict among team members. As evaluation criteria are often to a degree subjective, political skill to win support for one's ideas and initiatives becomes ever more vital.

The Scrum master is a good example of a new role in teams. It does not include much formal authority over team members, but Scrum masters are nevertheless supposed to influence and control the behavior of individuals enough to keep the process on track. The control they exert may be largely unobtrusive, but it inevitably involves the systematic use of power to influence the conduct of members in line with the needs of their teams, whether they cooperate or not.

Scrum masters also have the responsibility to remove impediments that block the progress of their teams. Their role usually does not grant them formal authority over stakeholders in organizations that affect their teams, which suggests that they need the ability to develop and leverage their informal power to address impediments effectively. It explains why Cohn (2009, p. 120) believes that Scrum masters should ideally have a degree of corporate political skill.

It is a fundamental part of the work as Scrum master to develop and use informal power in organizations to support teams. There are cases where Scrum masters use the same skill to dominate teams and obstruct self-organization, and the same can be said of agile coaches and product owners. In theory, it should not happen, and Scrum masters should act as servant leaders, but there is considerable evidence that it nevertheless occurs in practice.

While a lack of understanding of the role may contribute to abuses of power, the underlying motives will often also reflect the fact that Scrum masters in organizations are subject to the same performance pressures as other members. If they coach teams that eventually fail, their reputation will generally suffer too.

Their response to the risk of career damage may well be to become more directive to ensure that team members spend their time on the things that truly matter to the Scrum masters. Where this self-serving behavior occurs, it shows that servant leadership in organizations can certainly not be taken for granted. On the contrary, it appears unrealistic to believe that individuals who spend significant effort on becoming a Scrum master in their organizations can easily turn into selfless leaders who put their own career second.

The other team members are not powerless and can stage effective resistance to overbearing Scrum masters. It suggests that the relationship between Scrum masters and teams is, in practice, the result of more or less intensive political processes that continue throughout the lifetime of projects and teams.

Peer pressure plays a critical role in Scrum. In the example of the engineer Dave that we reviewed in Chapter 7, the team put significant pressure on a member. Before the Scrum master resolved the situation, his peers treated Dave poorly for several days. In Dave's case, the Scrum master stayed in control of the conflict and finally arranged a happy ending. The episode shows that peer pressure is the exercise of power, not least by Scrum masters. The instrumentalization of peer pressure in Scrum normalizes the use of power and likely increases the level of political activity in teams.

As the instances of political stakeholder behavior presented above show, Scrum has much potential for organizational politics. Because most of the power used by stakeholders in Scrum projects is informal, it is easy to overlook that power is exercised at all, and it is often difficult to understand how exactly it operates and what purpose it ultimately serves. Political actors amplify this effect because they routinely disguise their actions and deny their true motives.

While Scrum was chosen as an example here, organizational politics affects other software processes as well. In practice, political behavior is often difficult to recognize, but it is pervasive in software development, and stakeholders who ignore it or fail to recognize it early enough are at risk of misjudging situations and suffering disadvantages.

Political Skill

A central goal of this book is to increase the political skill of readers, and it naturally raises the question of what that actually means in practical terms. Answering the question is not as straightforward as one might think. Although scholars and practitioners have made many attempts to define the concept of political skill in the last 40 years, there is no single, generally accepted definition.

Buchanan and Badham (2020, ch. 9) provide a detailed overview of some noteworthy attempts to characterize the concept. They note that the most prominent approach is the model of political skill defined by the American academic Gerald Ferris and his team. However, they point out that it is relatively narrow and suggest putting additional emphasis on the role of political tactics and some other aspects.

In this book, we adopt a definition of political skill that takes Ferris' model as well as Buchanan and Badham's advice into account. It is based on the definition of political behavior presented in Chapter 1. Accordingly, we regard political skill as the ability of a stakeholder to use political behavior effectively and efficiently. In practical terms, it is the ability to develop and use power to achieve own goals in situations where disagreement and opposition are likely.

The definition is simple, straightforward and logical, but it is also unspecific, while the term "skill" implies something that is teachable and can be operationalized. It is necessary to characterize the concept of political skill in more concrete terms. At the same time, it is important to keep in mind that any such more specific characterization can only be an approximation. It will never include all abilities of humans that can potentially contribute to political skill, and a more realistic goal is to identify some essential aspects that dominate in most practical cases.

To better understand what political skill means in practice, it is helpful to look at the more concrete characterization offered by Fitzpatrick and Collins-Sussman (2015, p. 99):

> Most people work in dysfunctional corporate bureaucracies and need to employ certain manipulative techniques to get things done effectively. Some people call this politics; others call it social engineering.

This characterization suggests that political skill is the ability to use certain manipulative techniques. Fitzpatrick and Collins-Sussman (2015, ch. 5) describe and discuss several of these techniques. Three representative examples are:

- Asking for forgiveness rather than permission (p. 108)

- Managing upward (p. 111)

- Seeking powerful friends (p. 116)

We already mentioned the first of these techniques in Chapter 5. It is related to a quotation attributed to the American computer pioneer Grace Hopper. It reflects the experience that bureaucracies sometimes impose pointless restrictions that prevent members of organizations from carrying out important work in a timely and productive manner. Where bureaucracy is a pointless obstacle, it may be an effective option to ignore the restrictions and get the job done. The hope is that either the transgression will go unnoticed or that the results will justify the means, and the unauthorized actions will be praised rather than punished.

The second technique is essentially impression management. It reflects the reality that hard work and good results alone are often not enough for career progression and that "selling yourself" well can deliver huge benefits. For example, it is advisable to highlight achievements and spend enough time on activities likely to produce visible positive results. It does not mean to neglect less visible routine work, but spending too much time on it can make people look unproductive.

The third technique reminds us that powerful allies are valuable in most political processes and that a network of influential contacts is an asset. Job titles are not the only indicator of power in organizations, and careful attention to the ways how informal power operates in them is advisable. Accordingly, a network of contacts should include relevant individuals with formal as well as informal power.

Political techniques of the kind explained above are nothing extraordinary, and many publications cover them. There is no doubt that most people in organizations occasionally use them. Some may have acquired their knowledge from books and other written materials, but equally well, they may have witnessed the political behavior of others and learned from their observations. Regardless of the origin, knowledge of political techniques is undoubtedly an asset, and it can be concluded that it represents a critical aspect of political skill.

Fitzpatrick and Collins-Sussman (2015, pp. 108) warn that the manipulation techniques listed in their book can backfire if they are applied in inappropriate situations. For example, when they discuss the option to ask for forgiveness rather than permission, they urge their readers to make a careful assessment of whether they can get away with the transgression. They emphasize that a type of political behavior that works in one situation may nevertheless lead to a disaster in another. One reason for different outcomes is that some bosses react furiously to any challenge of their authority, while others are more relaxed about justifiable transgressions by their subordinates.

Pfeffer (2010, p. 15) voices a similar warning and criticizes that authors and speakers occasionally present political advice as universal truths, not least because many practitioners like to hear simple success formulas. He cautions that political techniques are based on probabilities and are not deterministic laws. It means that they can fail in a given situation even if cultural and personality factors appear to be a perfect match.

There is no doubt that the applicability of political techniques is always dependent on the context. Therefore, the ability to assess the organizational context and to choose the most appropriate technique is another critical aspect of political skill.

A third aspect of political skill can be inferred from the definition of the concept that Buchanan and Badham (2020, p. 35) adopt, which was essentially suggested by Gerald Ferris. It draws attention to the potential use of interpersonal skills to make target individuals more susceptible to manipulation. It requires a good understanding of the impressions, feelings, attitudes, and thoughts of others. By choosing a matching interaction and communication style, it may be possible to elicit desired reactions. One possible application is behavior that creates the appearance of sincerity, which may help to inspire trust in others. Individuals who trust another person are less likely to question the person's motives, and it works in favor of political actors who try to hide their true motives.

In summary, the concept of political skill adopted in this book can essentially be characterized by three aspects:

- Knowledge of political techniques: The ability to apply strategies, tactics, and other identifiable patterns of political behavior

- Understanding of the context: The ability to assess the organizational culture, the personalities of the affected individuals, and other situational factors

- Interpersonal skill: The ability to adopt an interaction and communication style that inspires desired reactions in others, in particular trust

Learning Politics

Not only is there widespread belief among professionals that political skill is beneficial for professional success, but there are also credible research studies that suggest the same. Naturally, it creates interest in organizational politics, and a large body of literature exists to satisfy it.

As organizational politics has been a field of systematic research since the 1960s, universities and other institutions regularly teach the subject. It may not play a prominent role in technical disciplines like computer science, but curricula related to advanced management studies usually cover the topic. In particular, organizational behavior, which is the study of human behavior in organizations, cannot reasonably be presented without significant attention to political behavior. Consequently, popular mainstream textbooks like Robbins and Judge (2019) dedicate at least a chapter to the study of power and politics.

Unlike academic textbooks, books targeting professionals are less concerned with theoretical explanations and focus on the practical skills needed to succeed in organizational politics. Fundamental to political skill is knowledge about strategies and tactics, and it is also what most professionals associate with effective political action. Therefore, it is no surprise that the authors of books on organizational politics for professionals often address the subject at one of two levels:

- Strategies
- Tactics

Authors who choose the level of strategies identify typical office politics problems that are caused by goal conflicts and affect individuals in organizations. For each of the problems, they suggest, describe, and discuss possible steps toward a solution, which essentially amounts to a generic, prescriptive strategy for tackling the problem. Books following this approach tend to be collections of such strategies, which readers have to adapt to the specific circumstances of their cases.

Dillon (2015) and Phipps and Gautrey (2005) are examples of books that address organizational politics at the level of strategies. In the following, we focus on Dillon's book for illustration. It contains 16 chapters in total, of which the first 12 chapters are each dedicated to a familiar office politics problem. Some representative examples are:

- Bosses who prioritize their career and do little for the careers of their subordinates (chapter 1)
- Control-freak bosses (chapter 3)

- Overly competitive peers (chapter 6)
- Powerful, exclusive cliques of peers (chapter 8)
- Managing disgruntled former peers (chapter 10)
- Protecting one's job during layoffs (chapter 12)

The first 12 chapters in Dillon's book have the same structure, each consisting of three main parts. The first part offers a general description of the problem, the second part explains why it occurs, and in the third part, Dillon describes and discusses possible measures to address it.

Books that approach office politics at the level of strategies tend to focus on practical advice and solutions. Usually, the authors devote a separate, self-contained chapter to each political problem and its suggested solution, simplifying the selective reading of chapters. A drawback of the approach is that any book can only cover a limited number of problems, inevitably leaving substantial gaps.

Authors who choose the level of tactics focus on types of behavior that are typically present in political processes. They tend to analyze every type in isolation to understand its purpose and how the behavior achieves it. The types of behavior are more or less sophisticated tactics. Books following this approach are primarily collections of tactics, which help readers identify, analyze, and understand political processes in general.

Pfeffer (1994, 2010), McIntyre (2005), and many other authors address organizational politics at the level of tactics. In the following, we focus on Pfeffer (1994). In his book, Pfeffer describes and explains several well-known tactics that occur in most political processes. Some representative examples are:

- Using resources and allies (chapter 5)
- Seeking access to information (chapter 6)
- Creating dependence (chapter 8)
- Framing issues (chapter 10)
- Manipulating information (chapter 13)

Pfeffer describes the tactics in detail, explains their functions, and makes suggestions on how political actors can use them effectively. He mainly presents theoretical deliberations based on academic research, which he supports with practical examples and anecdotes.

Books that approach office politics at the level of tactics primarily focus on the analysis of political processes. To this end, the authors identify a set of relevant tactics, which serves as an analytical toolkit. A limitation of the approach is that it focuses on a broad understanding of political processes rather than problem-solving, which has the consequence that most authors offer limited advice on strategy formulation.

The two book types address different reader needs. The first type is suitable for professionals who look for practical solutions to concrete problems they have in the workplace. The second type serves an audience that is interested in a general understanding of political processes in the workplace.

Political Ethics

Political behavior in organizations has an ambiguous reputation. On the one hand, it has a bad image and is associated with dishonest, cunning, devious, manipulative behavior, which is widely regarded as unacceptable. On the other hand, Buchanan and Badham (2020, pp. 34) observe, managers who admit political actions often give examples that sound much more positive. Frequently, they describe critical situations when they faced apathy or resistance in their organizations and had to engage in politics because there was no other way to make something beneficial happen.

Many managers hold the view that the use of political tactics, in the right circumstances, is a legitimate means to get work done. It is reflected in the writings of authors who regard political behavior that serves legitimate organizational goals as acceptable. For example, Dillon (2015) sees politics as a necessary evil but suggests that it does not have to end in destructive conflict. Instead, she argues (xii):

> It's about being *constructively* political—understanding personal dynamics among colleagues, working together for mutual advantage, and ultimately focusing on the good of the enterprise.

The statement represents a simple ethical position, which states that political behavior is justifiable if it is constructive. It means that the stakeholders cooperate to find conflict solutions that are mutually beneficial and ultimately advance organizational goals.

These considerations hint at two criteria that are central to ethics. One is the question of fairness, the other concerns utility. An action that creates an advantage for one stakeholder at another's expense without a justification may be unfair. One that overall only produces harm has no utility. Both outcomes appear highly undesirable, and it suggests that political behavior should at least be fair and have utility.

Utility and fairness are fundamental criteria in the ethical framework for organizational politics developed by the academics Gerald Cavanagh, Dennis Moberg, and Manuel Velasquez. It was first published in 1981, and Buchanan and Badham (2020, p. 70) note that it is current, despite its age. The framework integrates three fundamental ethical theories:

- Utilitarian theory
- Theory of rights
- Theory of justice

The evaluation of political behavior with the framework requires the assessment of the conditions defined by each of the three ethical theories. If it violates any of them without an overwhelming reason justifying the violation, it has to be rejected on ethical grounds. Otherwise, it is regarded as ethically justifiable.

Each of the three theories that Cavanagh et al. combine in their framework has strengths and weaknesses, which are extensively discussed in the literature on ethics. The three theories are included in the framework because they mutually compensate for their respective deficiencies. The goal is to create a balance where all of the most critical ethical considerations applying to political actions receive adequate attention.

It is not difficult to illustrate the weaknesses of the individual ethical theories. For example, according to the utilitarian theory, the most ethical action in a given situation is the one that delivers the most benefit for the stakeholders. At first glance, it may look like a compelling idea, but there is a serious drawback. The approach does not take the distribution of the benefits between the stakeholders into account. All that counts is to maximize the total benefit of all stakeholders taken together, and it does not matter if the resulting distribution of benefits between them is unfair.

The framework compensates for the lack of attention to the issue of fairness in utilitarian theory by combining it with a theory of justice. It requires that the allocation of benefits and costs that an action causes must be fair. Likewise, the theory of rights ensures that certain fundamental individual rights of humans are always respected.

The three theories in the framework can provide conflicting results. In such cases, if overwhelming reasons justify it, the framework explicitly permits the violation of the conditions imposed by any of the three theories. For example, if a political action satisfies the theories of rights as well as justice but fails to maximize the utility of the outcome, a less than optimal but still good enough level of utility may be acceptable. The option to make exceptions in extraordinary cases allows pragmatic trade-offs when decision-makers apply the framework.

Cavanagh et al.'s framework offers a straightforward integration of three fundamental, established, proven ethical theories. While it provides guidance for the evaluation of political actions, it does not reduce it to a mechanical exercise. Because Buchanan and Badham (2020, ch. 3) devote a chapter to political ethics and provide detailed coverage of the framework, we only look at some selected aspects in the following and highlight challenges that users of the framework face.

We use the observation that it is sometimes easier to ask for forgiveness than permission as an example. As noted earlier, it is a popular way to rationalize acting without permission, which writers like Mancuso (2014) and Fitzpatrick and Collins-Sussman (2015) describe in some detail. There are situations where the idea to act first and apologize later is appealing, but it is also clear that it may be hard to justify. Even if the trick succeeds, the question remains whether behaving in this way can be ethical.

For demonstration, we look at the following situation. It involves three individuals, A, B, and C, and B is the boss of A and C. B identifies a problem and asks A and C to forward ideas on how to solve it. A and C are equally qualified and work on the problem independently. When C finds a potential solution, C follows the instructions, prepares a proposal, sends it to B and waits for a response. At the same time, A finds a different solution but does not care about the instructions, implements it without permission, and only informs B and C afterwards. A's intention is to create facts that effectively force B to accept A's solution. The solutions found by A and C are equally good, and if B had to choose one, each would have a 50% chance to win.

If A's solution wins, A gains a utility of UA, likewise C gains a utility of UC if C's solution wins. B gains a utility of UB from the opportunity to choose between the solutions.

Using the framework for an ethical assessment, we start with the utilitarian theory. There are two options, either A acts without permission or A asks for permission. The total utility in the first case is UA, and the total expected utility in the second is $0.5 \times UA + 0.5 \times UC + UB$ because B would have the opportunity to choose, giving each solution a 50% chance. The theory requires comparing the two values, which turns out to be a critical issue.

It is necessary to establish a relationship between UA, UB, and UC to compare the values for the total utility in the two cases. One way to solve the problem is to assume UA = UB = UC. In this scenario, the total utility in the first case is UA, and in the second, it is $0.5 \times UA + 0.5 \times UC + UB = 2 \times UA$. It means that asking B for permission results in more overall utility. According to the utilitarian theory, the conclusion is that not asking B for permission is unethical and has to be rejected.

In the above analysis, we assume UA = UB = UC. We now change the assumption to UB = UC = 0.1 × UA. It means that being informed does not matter much to the boss and that C is less interested in the whole affair than A. In this scenario, the total utility of not telling B remains UA, but the total expected utility of telling B is now 0.5 × UA + 0.5 × UC + UB = 0.65 × UA. The changed assumption has the effect that asking B for permission results in less overall utility. According to the utilitarian theory, the conclusion is that not asking B for permission is not unethical and does not have to be rejected.

The second theory that A needs to take into account is the theory of rights, but to keep the example short, we skip it and go straight to the theory of justice. A central principle of the theory is distributive justice, meaning that the allocation of gains and losses among the stakeholders should be fair. In particular, individuals who do not differ in any relevant aspect should be treated similarly.

A's unauthorized implementation causes a distribution of gains and losses where A gains UA, while C gains nothing. The two different solutions found by A and C are equally good, and it does not justify rewarding A more than C. Arguably, A's unauthorized implementation does not justify the difference in rewards either. As there is no plausible reason to reward A and C differently, the theory of justice suggests that A's action is unethical and should be rejected.

In both scenarios, Cavanagh et al.'s framework rejects the idea to act first and apologize later as unethical. As a few authors mention the trick, suggesting that it is in widespread use, it is clear that the framework imposes far-reaching restrictions on political activities on ethical grounds. The restrictive nature of the framework is no accident because much practical political behavior in organizations is unquestionably not ethical by any conventional standard.

The framework requires assumptions, and as the two scenarios show, different assumptions can cause significantly different results. It is one of two fundamental problems with the framework Buchanan and Badham (2020, pp. 71) point out. As they explain, it is an issue of considerable practical importance because stakeholders in political processes routinely manipulate information in their favor, and one consequence is that it may be difficult for them to agree on the relevant assumptions.

The second problem Buchanan and Badham highlight is the notion of overwhelming reasons that may justify the violation of ethical norms in exceptional cases. There are compelling reasons why Cavanagh et al. added this flexibility to their framework, but it creates the problem to decide what counts as an overwhelming reason. Without a doubt, it is a question that invites interpretation and debate, and it may be difficult for stakeholders to find an agreement.

To illustrate the problem, we refer to the first scenario in the above example, which assumes UA = UB = UC. Based on the utilitarian theory, the conclusion is that not asking B for permission is unethical. Yourdon (2003, pp. 81) gives a good idea of what could be an overwhelming reason to ignore the rejection. He refers to death march projects that confront a project manager A with the moral dilemma to either violate bureaucratic rules imposed by the organization or risk project failure. If rational negotiations fail to resolve the dilemma, Yourdon concludes, it may be justifiable to act first and apologize later. Whether this justification is acceptable to B, however, can be doubted.

Cavanagh et al.'s framework provides useful guidance for the ethical assessment of political actions. It has weaknesses, though, and there is little to stop political actors from exploiting them to put a questionable seal of approval on their immoral activities to placate their conscience or mislead others. Even where stakeholders use the framework in good faith, there is a risk that they will sometimes be unable to agree on necessary assumptions or obtain questionable results.

These problems are not unique to the framework discussed here and apply to some degree to any method of ethical assessment. Any assessment depends on information and judgements, and both are inevitably affected by distorting influences like confirmation bias and motivated reasoning. Such effects can significantly change what appears acceptable or not. It shows that applied political ethics will never be a mechanical exercise but will always depend on honesty, reason, and reflexivity.

Political Analysis

Tactics are the basic unit of action in organizational politics, and consequently, they also play a central role in its analysis. Researchers and practitioners have made many attempts to describe and explain fundamental tactics and create lists of the most popular ones. These efforts have come from diverse backgrounds with different perspectives, and not all of the work was very systematic. It has led to a scattered, disjoint body of literature concerning tactics. In this chapter, we first present a simple analytical framework based on tactics, and subsequently, we provide a short overview of the related literature.

Analytical Framework

In this book, we essentially adopt a simplified version of Pfeffer's (1994) analytical framework. It consists of the following seven political tactics:

- Building power
- Limiting power
- Setting agendas

© Peter Wendorff 2022
P. Wendorff, *Politics in Software Development*,
https://doi.org/10.1007/978-1-4842-7380-7_9

- Framing issues
- Providing information
- Mobilizing support
- Creating commitment

We mean the above simplified analytical framework when we refer to "the framework" in the remainder of the book unless otherwise noted.

Political actors in organizations mostly employ these seven tactics to achieve their strategic goals. Additional tactics may be relevant in some cases, but we focus on the above seven in this book. The framework serves the purpose of drawing attention to stakeholder behavior that is characteristic of political processes. Because we will explain the tactics in detail in Chapter 10, we only provide a first overview in the following.

Building power: Political actors know that their success depends on power. They tend to make good use of opportunities to enhance it. Invariably, it involves impression management because the perception of it can be as effective as actual power. Attempts of stakeholders to increase their power mainly refer to one of its bases described in Chapter 2. For example, resources can be a potent base of power in organizations. By gaining exclusive control of critical resources, stakeholders can increase their power. Where they cannot gain control themselves, it may still be possible to achieve indirect access or influence by helping an ally gain control. In any case, a good relationship with people who have access to resources or control them can be very beneficial, which explains why networks of contacts are valuable resources in themselves.

Limiting power: Often, the absolute power of political actors is less relevant than the question of how much they have relative to their opponents. To change the power differential in their favor, they can either increase their own power or decrease that of opponents. The latter option usually targets the power bases described in Chapter 2. For example, questioning somebody's character, reputation, or expertise in public can potentially reduce the individual's power.

Setting agendas: Stakeholders in organizations benefit more or less from the status quo, and consequently, some try to change it while others resist change. An effective way to prevent change is to keep a contentious issue off the organizational agenda, which is the observation that led to the second dimension of power explained in Chapter 2. Change often requires the opposite and to put an issue on the agenda. Despite the theoretical background, it is also a problem of practical relevance. For example, stakeholders with a low level of power frequently find it difficult to gain attention for their ideas and concerns in organizations. One way for them to get their points on the organizational agenda is to ask a more powerful stakeholder to lobby on their behalf.

Framing issues: How issues are presented to individuals can significantly influence how they see and judge them. The proverbial application of the effect is the choice to call the same drinking glass half full, which sounds more positive, or half empty, which sounds more negative. In general, a frame is a context used to present facts, and it can activate certain perceptions, attitudes, thoughts, interpretations, images, and emotions in individuals, which may affect their judgement and reaction. Political actors often exploit the effect and carefully construct the frame in which they present an issue to elicit the response they want. For example, by highlighting parallels between a proposed project and a previous, similar, messy, failed project, it may be possible for them to activate negative associations in others. It can potentially bias the judgement of decision-makers and lead them to reject the project, even if they would approve it otherwise.

Providing information: Because it is often onerous and time-consuming to find, the consumers of information in organizations frequently rely on others to provide it. Inevitably, it gives the providers the opportunity to manipulate the information available to a given stakeholder at a given time. Providers can filter, amend, distort, invent, or otherwise modify it. Moreover, they can also leak it to unauthorized parties, and where they operate as gatekeepers, they can exclude selected stakeholders or provide partial information. Thus, they may be able to control when participants get involved in political processes, if at all, and how they judge issues. For example, by overstating the benefits of a project and downplaying its risks, it may be possible to mislead decision-makers into approving it. The effect can potentially be amplified by excluding its opponents from the information or releasing it when it suits advocates of the project.

Mobilizing support: In most organizations, it helps to know the right people and have a good relationship with them to get work done. Among the many advantages that networks of contacts can offer are unofficial access to information, ways around bureaucratic barriers, support for own ideas, and protection from people in authority. Undoubtedly, a network of contacts is a valuable resource, but the crucial step is to mobilize it effectively when help is needed. Support will often depend on friendship, personal liking, emotional dependence, or shared interests. Social exchange relationships are another mechanism to secure it. They operate on the principle of mutual obligation and the expectation that stakeholders will pay back favors. Support relationships can give rise to unlikely alliances. For example, it is not uncommon for a stakeholder to support an opponent to harm a common enemy.

Creating commitment: Once humans have publicly committed to an action, it often becomes more difficult for them to renege on it. One reason is that breaking the promise to act would make it look like an error of judgment. To avoid embarrassment, stakeholders will sometimes honor a previous commitment that is no longer in their interest. It is possible to exploit the effect for political ends. By encouraging insignificant, justifiable pledges at first, the goal is to start a series of slowly escalating commitments. The more resources are spent, the more difficult it becomes to reverse course and admit that the past actions were a waste of time or money. For example, to win approval for the purchase of a new software tool, its proponents may at first suggest trying out a free evaluation version. Once the free version is available, they may propose using it for a small, non-critical, internal project and finally for a larger project that requires buying the chargeable product. Because of the considerable time and effort already spent at this point, it will be difficult to deny the request and declare the experiment a failure.

Framework Development

In Chapter 4, we already presented a short overview of Pfeffer's (1994) analytical framework for organizational politics and explained how it relates to the three-dimensional view of power. As we already discussed the second and third dimensions of power in Part II of the book, we concentrate on the part of Pfeffer's framework that represents the first dimension. The relevant tactics are:

- Building power: Developing bases of formal and informal power (chapters 5 to 9)

- Framing issues: Constructing a particular perspective on a controversial issue to influence the judgment of others in favor of desired conclusions (chapter 10)

- Using interpersonal influence: Using social pressure, ingratiation, and the display of emotions to influence the behavior of others (chapter 11)

- Optimizing timing: Delaying issues or raising them at the right time to achieve desired outcomes (chapter 12)

- Manipulating information and its analysis: Using selected information and biased analysis (chapter 13)

In this book, we adopt the part of Pfeffer's framework shown above with six minor changes:

1. "Limiting power" is added

2. "Mobilizing support" is added

3. "Creating commitment" is added

4. "Using interpersonal influence" is removed

5. "Optimizing timing" is renamed to "setting agendas"

6. "Manipulating information and its analysis" is renamed to "providing information"

The first three changes add items to the list of tactics in the framework. The topics are all extensively covered by Pfeffer (1994), albeit less prominently, and in this sense, we only rearrange existing material and emphasize selected aspects.

The removed item is not needed because we regard the ability to exert interpersonal influence as a part of interpersonal skill, which is a central aspect of political skill, as explained in the previous chapter.

With changes no. 5 and 6, we rename items. We rename the item concerned with timing because we regard agendas as the key concept here. However, there is no question that good timing is essential for effective agenda-setting. Control over what gets on the organizational agenda is critical, but so is choosing the right moment. We rename the item concerned with information to make it more neutral, like the other labels used for tactics in the framework. The new name emphasizes that all information provided by stakeholders can influence political processes, regardless of whether they manipulate it or not.

The above six changes serve the purpose to make the framework adopted in this book more memorable and easier to use. It is not a criticism of Pfeffer's (1994) framework or an attempt to change it substantially.

The seven tactics in the framework are not in random order. Instead, each prepares the ones that follow it. If they are all executed in order, they represent a simple, generic campaign strategy, which comprises three phases that focus on specific aspects:

1. Power

2. Issue

3. Action

As power is the basis of political action, in the first phase, the focus is on building own power and limiting that of opponents. In the second phase, the focus shifts to the issue motivating the campaign. It is necessary to put it on the agenda, frame it, and provide information supporting the frame. In the third phase, the focus is on action. Actions include the mobilization of supporters and steps that commit others to the desired outcome.

It is important to note that the linear order that the three phases imply is an idealized view for instructional purposes. It rarely resembles the actual political behavior of stakeholders in political processes, which is usually not linear and more complex.

Related Work

The field of organizational politics has attracted considerable interest from academics as well as practitioners. Consequently, there are alternatives to choosing Pfeffer's (1994) work as the basis for the analytical framework developed in the previous section. In this section, we briefly look at eight potential alternatives. The eight sources serve as examples and represent a good overview of the related literature. We briefly characterize the sources and explain the reasons why Pfeffer's work is the best choice for our purposes. The sources are:

- Three textbooks: Robbins and Judge (2019), Handy (1999), Buchanan and Badham (2020)

- One academic book: Mintzberg (1983)

- One academic journal article: Sabherwal and Grover (2010)

- Three professional books: Fitzpatrick and Collins-Sussman (2015), Simmons (1997), and McIntyre (2005)

The sources were selected based on their quality and diversity. They represent a broad overview of the relevant literature on organizational politics. Seven are books, and one is a journal article. The books are leading titles and contain at least a chapter dedicated to organizational politics. Each provides a list of political tactics that the authors regard as particularly relevant. The journal article is about political processes in information systems development and is from a leading academic journal.

It may be surprising that the sources do not include Yourdon's (2003) title *Death March*. The reason is that Yourdon does not identify a set of political tactics in his book. Where he discusses politics, the focus is usually on practical advice for managers on how to solve concrete problems rather than a systematic exploration of the role tactics play in the solutions. For example, when he discusses "negotiation strategies" (pp. 76), he describes typical scenarios that managers may face and discusses potential ways to deal with them but makes no attempt to explain how his suggestions relate to tactics.

We also do not include Rollinson's (2008) textbook in the list of eight sources, although it contains a chapter on power, politics, and conflict that presents two separate lists of tactics. The reason is that Rollinson takes the lists from Mintzberg (1983) and Pfeffer (1981) without adding much to the original material. As Mintzberg (1983) is among the sources and Pfeffer (1994) builds on Pfeffer's earlier title, there is no need to include Rollinson's book.

We start the literature overview with the three textbooks. All offer lists of tactics, but only Handy (1999, pp. 306) describes them in enough detail. Nevertheless, it is still far less detailed than the material in Pfeffer (1994). It is not surprising because Pfeffer's entire book is about the presentation of a framework based on tactics for the analysis of organizational politics, while the subject is usually only one of many in textbooks.

Mintzberg (1983) has been an enormously influential work on stakeholder power and organizational politics. The book includes detailed descriptions of 13 "games" (pp. 187) that stakeholders in organizations play in pursuit of their goals. Some of the games represent well-known tactics. A drawback is that Mintzberg does not provide much insight into how the games are related. The list of games is interesting, but the material in Pfeffer (1994) is much better integrated.

Sabherwal and Grover's (2010) journal article is about a specific empirical research project that aims to identify political processes typical of information systems development projects. Interestingly, they cite neither Mintzberg (1983) nor Pfeffer (1981, 1994) and prefer to develop an analytical framework of eight political tactics based on other sources. Understandably, they specifically design their framework for the analysis of their data set, but it raises concerns that it may not apply very well in different circumstances. In comparison, Pfeffer (1994) represents a universal approach and is not shaped by the needs of a single study.

We end the overview with the three professional books. Fitzpatrick and Collins-Sussman (2015) describe a selection of strategies and tactics, but there is no suggestion that the list is in any sense complete. Simmons (1997) identifies ten "games," which are mainly well-known tactics. Most of them appear to be destructive and either damage the power base of opponents or attempt to disrupt their activities. Without a doubt, her choice of tactics is skewed toward negative political behavior. McIntyre (2005) provides a more systematic and balanced view than the two other sources. She presents detailed descriptions of several tactics, but she does not link them to relevant theories or research. The same criticism applies to the two other sources. In general, all three pay little attention to independent research, which limits their credibility. In this respect, Pfeffer (1994) follows a different approach and carefully links the material presented in his book to independent, credible research.

In summary, the comparison with the eight sources above highlights some characteristics of Pfeffer's (1994) approach that make it particularly suitable for the purposes of this book. His framework is well documented, integrated, universal, and credible. For these reasons, we choose it as the basis of the framework adopted in this book.

Evaluation and Limitations

Different authors have documented many diverse tactics, strategies, and other prescriptions. There is some agreement on basic tactics, but there are also substantial differences. A consequence is that there is no generally accepted list of political tactics.

The lack of agreement on tactics has several reasons. One is the freedom to define tactics at different levels of abstraction and detail. A good example is Handy's (1999, p. 307) decision to treat the control and distortion of information as two distinct tactics, while most other authors do not distinguish them. Both choices are justifiable, and which option is more suitable ultimately depends on the application context. Sometimes the distinction may make sense, and sometimes it may just add unnecessary detail.

Another reason for differences is that all authors develop their lists of tactics based on literature reviews, empirical research, personal experiences, the target audience, and other factors. There can be crucial differences in the literature authors read, how they collect and interpret data, their personal experiences, and their target audience. For example, Pfeffer (1994) comes from a different professional background than McIntyre (2005), and Sabherwal and Grover (2010) certainly have other priorities than the author of a book for professionals.

Because there is no agreement on tactics, choosing Pfeffer's (1994) framework in this book is, to some extent, an arbitrary decision. However, it is clear that it has several desirable properties that make it a justifiable choice and solid foundation.

A limitation of Pfeffer's framework is a lack of attention to the systematic development of strategies. For example, there is little information on how political actors combine tactics to form effective strategies. The limitation is characteristic of approaches to organizational politics that, like Pfeffer's analysis, operate at the level of tactics. The weakness is not specific to his work and more or less applies to all of the eight sources reviewed in the previous section. Readers need to be aware that the same limitation applies to this book.

The framework adopted in this book has a second limitation, which does not apply to Pfeffer's framework. Unlike Pfeffer, we do not regard the use of interpersonal skills as a tactical option and do not provide a detailed analysis of the skills in this book. The lack of attention to these skills may be surprising because, at the same time, we recognize them as a central aspect of political skill. The main reason for not covering them in detail is that they are a core subject in many other books related to politics, including Dillon (2015), McIntyre (2005), and Pfeffer (1994, 2010). Moreover, all professionals benefit from better interpersonal skills, and there is no shortage of good literature on the subject.

The framework helps analyze political behavior by suggesting what to look out for in stakeholder activities. It provides a political context for behavior that may look innocent when seen in isolation but is more likely indicative of well-known tactics. In Chapter 10, we will discuss the tactics in the framework in more detail and use them to highlight political behavior in software development.

Political Tactics

Members of organizations routinely use political behavior to advance their interests. Because politics is a normal part of life in organizations, their members may not even perceive instances of popular tactics as political behavior. In this chapter, we explain the framework's seven tactics in detail and show how stakeholders apply them in software development.

Building Power

In Chapter 2, we described four important bases of power in organizations:

- Positions
- Expert knowledge
- Resources
- Personal characteristics

Members of organizations can systematically develop each of the four bases to increase their power through career planning, training, and political activities like networking. Positions not only provide formal authority, but they also come with specific opportunities that Handy (1999, p. 128) calls "invisible assets," which in most cases are related to information, networking, and the social environment. Individuals can exploit them to gain access to valuable information, network with influential individuals, or influence the work environment. These informal activities can result in considerable power beyond the official job description.

© Peter Wendorff 2022
P. Wendorff, *Politics in Software Development*,
https://doi.org/10.1007/978-1-4842-7380-7_10

In political processes, informal power can be particularly effective because opponents may not be aware of it and miss opportunities to timely intervene when it is used. A typical case is a political actor with informal access to a decision-maker, opening up the possibility to influence decisions before they officially reach the organizational agenda. Issues may already be decided behind closed doors when they become matters of broader consultation and debate. It can reduce the official decision process to a formality and deny other stakeholders meaningful participation in decisions (Rollinson 2008, p. 402).

Control over a resource on which others depend can give a stakeholder power, but the strength of the effect varies because the resource may be essential in one situation but not another. Three factors that produce dependency on something are its importance, scarcity, and substitutability. A stakeholder with control over a resource that other parties need, which is also hard to find or replace with something else, has significant power over them. It explains why gatekeepers can gain enormous power. Because they are the only way to access a resource, others who need it depend on them (Robbins & Judge 2019, pp. 392).

The systematic development of power is a core subject in all practical books on organizational politics, and research convincingly shows that it has a strong positive effect on career progress, which is hardly a surprise. Nevertheless, many members of organizations spend little time on it. Using the example of networking, Pfeffer (2010, p. 113) speculates that many shy away from purely instrumental relationship building because they regard it as distasteful. He sees a tendency to overestimate the impact of good work on career progress as another reason.

A third reason Pfeffer cites is that it usually takes time and effort to build a powerful position in organizations and that individuals may think it is not worth the cost. It can be a dangerous belief because a lack of power may only become visible when a conflict arises where it is needed. At that point, it may be too late to acquire the power necessary for effective political action, creating the risk of serious harm. Therefore, the question is not whether it is needed but how much is appropriate and how to acquire and develop it efficiently.

The effectiveness of the four bases of power depends on the perception and judgment of others, who not only take objective facts into account that are clear and can be verified but also depend on less objective information. Through its careful management, stakeholders can create the appearance that they are more or less powerful or produce other wrong impressions. It may give them influence over other parties in a political process. A case in question are persons who succeed in creating a false impression of trustworthiness. It increases the likelihood that others will fall victim to false promises they would never take seriously otherwise.

Robbins and Judge (2019, p. 408) define impression management as the conscious attempt to influence the perceptions of others to control the image that they have of the impression manager. The definition does not require the resulting image to be untrue, although, in reality, it will usually be distorted and highlight some aspects rather than others.

Impression management may allow manipulating other stakeholders, which underscores its central role in political processes. Members of organizations routinely practice it, and as Rollinson (2008, p. 123) remarks, it is one of the reasons for the continuing popularity of the most famous manual on impression management, Dale Carnegie's bestseller *How to Win Friends and Influence People*. Remarkably, more than 80 years after its publication, Carnegie's book remains popular.

Robbins and Judge (2019, p. 409) highlight three broad categories of impression management:

- Self-focused
- Defensive
- Assertive

The first form is a core topic in virtually any book on office politics, and a typical example is what Fitzpatrick and Collins-Sussman (2015, p. 111) call to "manage upward." They remind their readers how important it is to create awareness of their contributions to ensure their bosses have a good impression of them. In general, self-focused impression management attempts to associate an actor with positive qualities. It includes activities like highlighting strengths, downplaying weaknesses, calling attention to achievements, and favorably comparing oneself to others.

Defensive techniques reactively try to avoid negative impressions and usually consist of excuses and apologies. Excuses are an attempt to avoid responsibility for a problem by presenting mitigating circumstances, while apologies admit some degree of culpability and seek a pardon in exchange for the display of remorse.

Assertive techniques proactively try to generate positive impressions. They include discretionary activities that make an individual appear more dedicated than required by volunteering for extra work or doing work much better than needed. Another form is ingratiation, which is behavior that aims to increase a target person's liking. It includes flattery, doing favors, or feigning agreement.

Professional qualifications are a popular area of impression management because they can confer considerable expert status. Martin (2020, pp. 143) notes that some questionable certifications for software professionals exist that can be obtained with minimal effort and only guarantee that the participants have paid a fee. For outsiders, it is often difficult to judge the value of a qualification, leaving much room for exaggerated claims.

Qualifications are not the only factor that affects the expert power of stakeholders. Another is how successfully they used it in the past. Experts whose solutions regularly cause unnecessary problems will, over time, lose the expert status and the associated power. In general, the unsuccessful use of power bases makes them less effective, while successful use reinforces them.

Because a reputation built on past success is a source of influence for experts, Buchanan and Badham (2020, pp. 26) suggest to treat it as a separate base of power. The idea is not helpful, and it is much more straightforward to keep in mind that qualifications are only one indicator of expertise. Another one is successful work, which does not necessarily depend on formal qualifications. Expert power based on expertise reflects both qualifications and reputation.

Reputation does not only matter in the case of expert power. Instead, the strength of any power base also depends on the record of stakeholders in the past. Consequently, the public perception of past behavior is frequently the target of impression management. Techniques like excuses and apologies are an example because they primarily serve to protect the reputation of stakeholders who bear some responsibility for past mistakes. By reducing reputational damage, they also shield the corresponding bases of power from harm.

Impression management works because it sends a message that may well be true. As long as it is plausible, target persons find it hard to detect the use of impression management, and when they have no reason for suspicion, they usually do not take the time to verify the veracity of a message. Their attitude quickly changes when they perceive the behavior as dishonest. The same behavior can be received in very different ways depending on whether it appears sincere or not. When targets of impression management sense manipulation, they usually reject it and become defensive (Robbins & Judge 2019, p. 408).

Limiting Power

The power of potential opponents and ways to curb it are major concerns in conflicts. The four bases described in Chapter 2 are the key to limiting it in the same way as they are the key to building power. The power of opponents is highly relevant because it is usually the power differential between stakeholders rather than the absolute level that determines the outcomes of political processes. Stakeholders can change the differential in their favor by either increasing their own power or decreasing that of opponents. In the following, we highlight some options to limit the power of individuals.

While it is rarely a realistic option to remove an individual from a position, it is sometimes possible to reduce the associated opportunities to amass informal power. One way is to create rules that prevent unofficial activities and create more transparency. Martin (2020, p. 143) effectively suggests this approach to limit the power of agile coaches. Accordingly, a possible rule could ban agile coaches from discussing the project schedule with management or making commitments on behalf of teams. Another plausible rule is his suggestion to rotate the coach role.

Expert knowledge is a highly regarded base of power, but it is also vulnerable to derogatory comments that question the legitimacy and credibility of the claim to expertise. Martin's (2020, pp. 143) criticism of questionable certifications demonstrates the effect. It likely has the consequence that at least some of his readers will treat such qualifications with skepticism, limiting their potential to generate power.

The dependency on resources that opponents control is a fundamental cause of weakness. A straightforward way to limit the effect is to reduce the need for the resources. In some cases, it may be possible to reduce it by doing things oneself or finding suitable alternative sources. For instance, in the case of gatekeepers, it may be possible to create new ways to access the resources. Alternatively, if the existing organizational controls appear too restrictive, lobbying for their relaxation may be a realistic option to reduce the influence of gatekeepers.

The resources available to individuals in organizations are limited. As they are a base of power, it is sometimes possible to gain an advantage by wasting the resources of opponents or diverting them away. It is often particularly effective to waste the time of others by creating uncertainty or unnecessary extra work. Possible actions include:

- Delaying information and action
- Being unreliable and unpredictable
- Providing vague or misleading information

- Intentionally misunderstanding messages
- Not acting as agreed to create confusion
- Insisting on unnecessary bureaucracy

Because individuals subjected to these actions can never be sure about the current work status, they constantly have to spend extra time on clarifying it or dealing with subtle errors. Simmons (1997, ch. 8, 9) dedicates two chapters to this kind of destructive behavior. As she explains, it is most effective if the target persons are unaware of its malicious intent and there is no open conflict. However, even if victims become suspicious, it is usually not difficult for the political actors to portray their obstruction as genuine misunderstandings and mistakes to avoid escalation and consequences.

Similar to expert knowledge, power based on personal characteristics is vulnerable to discrediting remarks. Simmons (1997, ch. 10) devotes a chapter to such attacks and observes that they are often disguised as innocent jokes, teasing, banter, or irony to avoid confrontation and create plausible deniability. While each on its own may not appear serious, attacks of this kind are often incessant, and the old proverb "[f]ling enough dirt and some will stick" provides the rationale behind them. Usually, the goal is to cast doubt on the character of individuals by suggesting that they are stupid, careless, lazy, unreliable, unreasonable, selfish, or untrustworthy. To the extent that character assassination affects perceptions, it can significantly lower the power of target persons.

Setting Agendas

It can take time for organizations to realize that a solution that worked in the past may no longer be adequate and that substantial change is necessary. In many, strong forces favoring the status quo exist and are only too willing to dismiss alternative ideas. There are multiple reasons for organizational inertia, and one of them is that meaningful change in many cases affects the distribution of power among stakeholders. Those who benefit from the status quo are naturally reluctant to give up any of their influence or privileges. It means that stakeholders who realize the need for change first often find it hard to win attention for their concerns and ideas.

Mancuso (2014, pp. 199) presents a detailed example of an organization in which a software architect made many critical technical decisions on behalf of teams. As he describes the case, the architect had the authority to make the decisions but showed little interest in their practical consequences and was not held accountable. Some of the outcomes were poor and led to problems for which blame went to the development teams, although they had no say in the decision process. According to Mancuso, the architect was unwilling to discuss changes to the process, and there was no other, obvious way for the developers to bring the issue on the organizational agenda.

Mancuso belonged to one of the affected teams. As he recounts, its members became increasingly frustrated that the software architect was responsible for critical technical decisions while the developers were held accountable for the problems the decisions caused. Eventually, the team secretly started to use a different web framework for development than the architect had chosen. It took the architect some time to notice the unauthorized use of the framework, but when he found out, he confronted Mancuso about it. It started a heated debate between the two that ended with an agreement to change the decision process and give teams more discretion to choose the tools for their work.

Mancuso's anecdote describes how a team violated an organizational rule to force a debate about the responsibility and accountability for technical decisions. The transgression came at the price of open conflict and was undoubtedly a risky move. However, after the architect had successfully stonewalled all attempts to discuss its concerns, it was one of the few options left to the team. With the benefit of hindsight, it was a savvy political move because once the issue was on the organizational agenda, a debate was inevitable. It allowed the stakeholders to engage in a necessary, overdue, productive political process to resolve the matter.

The case clearly illustrates the importance of agenda-setting in organizations. As Pfeffer (1981, p. 147) explains, the ability to get contentious, formerly ignored issues on the agenda is critical because it enables political processes that otherwise would not take place. Once they start, the political processes provide arenas where stakeholders can clarify their positions, challenge opposing viewpoints, find supporters, and engage in negotiations.

Because it allows to block political processes, control of the agenda is an essential weapon in the struggle for power in organizations, Pfeffer concludes. It is, of course, the observation that motivated the debate that gave rise to the second dimension of power described in Chapter 2.

The central role of the agenda in power struggles is also the primary reason why those in positions of power institutionalize practices in organizations that strictly limit meaningful participation in agenda-setting to a select few. The restrictive practices become the rules of the game and embedded in organizations, and often they are so much taken for granted that disadvantaged stakeholders do not even consider a challenge.

Pfeffer (1994, ch. 12) provides many examples showing that good timing is a critical success factor in agenda-setting. Bringing up an issue for political debate without a clear plan on how to succeed in it is usually a bad idea. Agenda-setting is not only about what is put on the agenda but also about when it happens.

Mancuso's anecdote illustrates good timing. The team waited for the architect to discover the transgression, and by then, it would have been expensive to reverse it. Moreover, there was already positive user feedback for the team's work, and slowing it down would have been unpopular with influential stakeholders. It put the architect in a difficult position, and it appears that he was angry and ill-prepared when he confronted Mancuso, who, without a doubt, was very well prepared and only waiting for the clash to happen.

In general, political actors regularly try to put issues on the agenda when the opposition cannot effectively respond because somebody is away, sick, on holiday, distracted, misled, not informed, or unprepared. If they succeed, they use the opportunity and try to push through their political plans, often with the goal to create facts that are difficult and costly to reverse. One reason is that the predominant attitude in many organizations is to move on and simply accept the facts, even if they are the result of unfair or illegitimate practices, as Pfeffer observes.

Timing also matters because there are more or less propitious moments for raising issues in organizations. The interest of stakeholders in a topic naturally depends on the circumstances. Changing circumstances can substantially alter their willingness to pay attention to a topic. In particular, a crisis can be an ideal opportunity to put an issue on the organizational agenda. For example, it is undoubtedly much easier to get attention for measures to improve information security after a breach.

The organizational agenda is constantly contested because diverse stakeholders compete for limited space and lobby to add their favorite demands. As software developers tend to have limited clout in organizations, it is no surprise that Fitzpatrick and Collins-Sussman (2015, pp. 109) offer some advice to them on practical agenda-setting. They suggest two possible approaches to put an idea on the agenda of an organization.

The first is similar to what Mancuso's anecdote describes. It consists of secretly implementing the idea at the grassroots level to demonstrate its value and create broad support. Once a substantial support base of actual users has developed, they note, it becomes difficult for management to ignore the idea or dismiss it.

The second technique is a more cautious approach and what most members of organizations would intuitively try. Fitzpatrick and Collins-Sussman call it "[p]ersuasion by proxy" (p. 110). It consists of talking about an idea to other members to raise awareness. The hope is to arouse interest in the subject and that, over time, it will become a talking point that eventually reaches the relevant decision-makers and gets their attention. If it happens, influential individuals may dominate the final stages of the persuasion effort, meaning that its originators may receive little credit, Fitzpatrick and Collins-Sussman warn.

Mancuso's anecdote and Fitzpatrick and Collins-Sussman's advice indicate the challenge for less influential members to get their concerns on the agenda of organizations. Influential stakeholders usually dominate it, requiring creativity and courage to succeed. Especially for ambitious individuals, it is of practical importance because they naturally question the status quo and seek attention for their ideas.

Framing Issues

If human decision behavior were purely rational, the choice of words used to represent information about decision alternatives should not matter as long as the information is logically equivalent. Likewise, adding irrelevant information to the decision process should not make a difference. Countless studies convincingly show that these expectations are often not met in practice due to a phenomenon called "framing." Researchers have paid particular attention to two forms of it, equivalence and emphasis framing (Chong & Druckman 2007).

In equivalence framing, the same alternatives are expressed using different language that is logically equivalent. The choice behavior of a purely rational decision-maker should not be affected by the mere change in wording. However, in practice, the choice of words strongly influences which alternatives the decision-makers prefer.

In emphasis framing, the information about alternatives is combined with additional, unnecessary information. Even if decision-makers do not need the latter, they usually do not entirely ignore it either. It can influence the mental representations on which they base their decisions, significantly impacting their choice of alternatives.

Emphasis framing works because the set of criteria that decision-makers use to evaluate alternatives is usually not fixed. Instead, they are often aware of many potential criteria, of which only a subset plays an active role at a given point in time. For a criterion to be activated, it needs to reach a certain threshold level of awareness. Because information can draw attention to some of them and omit others, it can also cause changes to the subset of active criteria and the resulting decision behavior (Chong & Druckman 2007).

In what follows, we will focus on emphasis framing because it is simple, effective, and plays a central role in political processes. Political actors can use it to set the context in which information is evaluated by promoting a particular frame that emphasizes certain aspects of an issue and obscures others. The fundamental premise behind this approach is that there are often various, justifiable criteria to judge a complex issue and that individuals have some freedom in choosing the ones they prefer. Framing involves the use of inconspicuous cues to influence how they exercise their freedom.

When political actors promote a frame, it is, of course, not just some arbitrary collection of criteria. Instead, it usually constitutes a carefully selected set that encourages individuals to look at an issue in a particular way and interpret information along certain lines of thinking. As Pfeffer (1994, p. 203) points out, it can give a political actor significant influence over the judgment and decisions of others who adopt the frame, making it a potent means for the exercise of power.

Ripley and Miller (2020, pp. 100) present an anecdote demonstrating the consequences of unsuitable framing. When one of them was asked by his boss to explain Scrum, he explained technical, theoretical details that were of little relevance to his boss. Predictably, the boss rejected the suggestion to use Scrum, and, with the benefit of hindsight, Ripley and Miller admit that the decision was understandable and the result of inadequate framing. It would have been better to frame Scrum in terms of business value rather than technology to convince the boss, they conclude.

A basic example of practical emphasis framing is the statement "Scrum provides frequent feedback through short iterations," which invokes a technical frame. Its appeal to a non-technical audience is likely limited because it does not refer to criteria on which business people typically focus.

The same sentence will likely invoke a somewhat different frame if it is preceded with a sentence like "Businesses need to be responsive." Although the first sentence does not say anything about Scrum, it creates the context for the second. It emphasizes responsiveness and thus activates the concept in the minds of readers. The heightened awareness of responsiveness presumably makes it easier for a non-technical audience to link Scrum's focus on frequent feedback to a criterion that directly matters to the business. If individuals adopt the business frame, their reaction to the ideas behind Scrum will likely be more positive.

Emphasis framing is one of the most widely used tactics in organizations. It is often employed to promote something by linking it to something else with a positive connotation. Examples are (Buchanan & Badham 2020, p. 22):

- Casting issues as organizational priorities
- Highlighting how ideas benefit the business

- Bundling concerns with related ones that receive attention
- Describing initiatives as unmissable opportunities

Of course, emphasis framing can also create negative associations. Meyer's (2014, p. 23, 31) observation that some authors try to give the wrong impression that plan-driven software processes are, in principle, variants of the much-criticized waterfall process can serve as an example. He presents two instances from books for illustration, but they are just simplistic misrepresentations that do not involve framing.

However, framing can create an association between plan-driven processes and the waterfall in the minds of readers in a less questionable way. Including an ostensibly innocent phrase like "The best-known plan-driven process is the waterfall process" in a text on software processes might have the desired effect. In the minds of some readers, the mere mentioning of the waterfall process will likely cause alarm and favor a more critical mental representation, achieving the goal of "[s]lander by association" (p. 23), as Meyer calls it.

While it works in a wide range of situations, the effectiveness of emphasis framing depends on several factors. Frames influence individuals more if they perceive them as relevant and do not hold deep, contradictory beliefs. If competing stakeholders in a political process employ framing to advance their goals, multiple frames compete with one another for legitimacy and dominance. While the competition reduces the effect of any single frame, in principle, framing continues to work in these conditions. It suggests that stakeholders who fail to engage in effective framing risk serious disadvantages (Chong & Druckman 2007).

Providing Information

Decisions critically depend on information, which explains its central role in organizations. Decision-makers have a vital interest in timely access to the best possible information because it allows them to spot opportunities and make the right decisions. They cannot take it for granted because significant decisions in organizations frequently require input from multiple stakeholders, who may seek their own advantage.

Providers of information can exploit the dependence on their input in two fundamental ways. First, they can influence decisions in line with their goals by manipulating information. To this end, stakeholders in organizations routinely filter, amend, distort, invent, or modify information they supply to others. Moreover, they can also omit information completely, hide it in an overwhelming amount of pointless data, or leak it to third parties. Second, dependency may give providers bargaining power. The more critical and exclusive the information is they can offer, the more can they trade it for benefits and favors like privileged access to influential individuals or valuable resources.

A case study of an information gatekeeper by Rost and Glass (2011, p. 22) demonstrates that the ability to withhold information can create an enormously powerful position. It took place at a company that had decided to offshore some software development activities to reduce costs. The transition heavily depended on the cooperation of a middle manager whose job the project threatened. Unsurprisingly, the manager made every effort to slow down the transfer of necessary information and ensured it was of low quality, citing a lack of time as justification. As a result, the project made little progress, and when it became clear that it was a pointless waste of money, the company finally cancelled it.

To find out what went wrong, the company conducted an investigation, which identified "incomplete and inadequate requirements" (p. 22) as the cause of the failure. The conclusion in the report is not even completely wrong, as Rost and Glass point out, because the state of the requirements documentation was undoubtedly poor. At the same time, the conclusion is misleading because it does not recognize the manager's self-interested obstruction of the requirements process as the root cause. The inability to identify the real cause of the failure indicates the powerful position of the information gatekeeper. Not only was he able to kill the project, but he could also successfully cover his tracks.

The relationship between power and access to information in organizations is bi-directional, and a change in one of them will usually lead to a corresponding change in the other. Those with higher positions have more rights concerning information, and they often amplify power differences through additional restrictions on information flows. A case in question is Fitzpatrick and Collins-Sussman's (2015, p. 103) observation that managers sometimes deny their subordinates access to relevant information to keep them in check. It may harm motivation and productivity, but acting as gatekeepers is a simple way for managers to maintain and reinforce their relevance and influence.

The critical role of information in organizations is all but a secret. Organizations underscore the importance of information-sharing through rules, procedures, sanctions, and incentives, and behavior compromising these efforts for selfish reasons is widely regarded as unacceptable. To avoid criticism and a feeling of guilt, individuals who engage in such behavior regularly invent reasons to make it appear beneficial or even necessary.

Yourdon (2003, pp. 46) presents a typical example when he notes that managers sometimes tell software developers not to talk to the users directly, although that can be highly beneficial for their work. As he observes, there is no shortage of excuses for such instructions, and one of the more popular is the claim that the developers do not understand the politics of the project and that direct contact could cause unnecessary political trouble. Whether such excuses are believable or not, they put managers in control of essential information and increase their power at the expense of the other stakeholders.

Most individuals who engage in controversial behavior use various excuses and rationalizations to make their behavior look acceptable to themselves and others. Typical reasons given for withholding relevant information are (Simmons 1997, ch. 5):

- Higher organizational goals make disclosure problematic
- Sharing is too complicated and time-consuming
- The information is most likely irrelevant
- Misunderstandings might cause harm
- The other side has not asked for the specific information
- Withholding is justifiable revenge for some wrongdoing of the other side
- Everybody here does it one way or the other

Because there are situations where these reasons may, at least in part, be plausible, it is often hard to detect and virtually impossible to prove if individuals manipulate information for political ends. Political actors can almost always claim that they just made an innocent mistake and deny allegations that they acted in bad faith.

Stakeholders usually only manipulate some of the relevant information but not all, which is another reason why politics concerning information frequently goes undetected at first. It creates the appearance that they cooperate, making it less likely that their victims will become suspicious. But even if the victims suspect political motives behind persistent communication problems, it is often so onerous and time-consuming to verify all aspects of complex information that it may not be a practical option to do so.

The detection of manipulated information is also challenging because it may be difficult to distinguish between the fair use of discretion that is part of a job and deliberate manipulation that is not. Pfeffer (1994, pp. 247) makes this point when he notes that there is often no single right way to look at data when problems in organizations are analyzed, and consequently, there is often no single correct answer to questions. Instead, the analysis of data usually involves some degree of judgment, which may be controversial. Whether a selection of data sources is comprehensive and balanced enough or not or a data analysis method sufficiently thorough and unbiased or not is often hard to tell. Inevitably, it leaves a gray zone that political actors can exploit with little risk of detection.

Mobilizing Support

Stakeholders pursuing their goals in organizations will, sooner or later, affect other stakeholders and need to win their support to be successful. It raises the question as to what techniques stakeholders can use to win support from others for their goals. The answer certainly depends on their level of formal authority. Superior parties can, at least in principle, impose their will on others, whereas stakeholders with less formal power need to find alternative ways to win support for their goals.

However, even where reliance on authority is an option, it may not be the most effective choice, and the question remains what other options there are. The question gains relevance by the proliferation of self-organizing teams in software development in recent years. They enjoy significant discretion to organize their work themselves, and members who have ideas for improvements need to win support for them.

As Mancuso (2014, ch. 14) is a strong advocate of self-organizing teams, it is no surprise that he devotes an entire chapter to ways how team members can influence peers and superiors. His observations illustrate from a practical perspective how individuals without relevant formal authority can still drive technical change by developing other bases of power. It is a vital skill for developers, he argues, because without, there is a risk that they know what is wrong in their projects but do not know how to change it. In particular, to drive change in political and bureaucratic environments, developers need more than just technical skills to achieve impact, Mancuso makes clear.

Influence behavior plays a central role in organizations and has been the subject of extensive academic research. A study by the academics David Kipnis, Stuart Schmidt, and Ian Wilkinson, published in 1980, identified eight influence types. It gained much attention, and in the years after its publication, many other researchers validated and refined the list of tactics. The American academic Gary Yukl played a central role in these efforts and is the main contributor to the list of nine influence tactics cited in Robins and Judge (2019, p. 395):

- Legitimacy: Relying on formal authority

- Rational persuasion: Presenting logical arguments based on factual evidence

- Inspirational appeals: Appealing to feelings, values, or aspirations to create enthusiasm and emotional commitment

- Consultation: Allowing individuals to participate in details of decisions or their implementation to foster a sense of ownership and accountability

- Exchange: Offering rewards in exchange for compliance

- Personal appeals: Appealing to friendship or loyalty

- Ingratiation: Doing favors, using flattery, showing sympathy and other friendly behavior

- Pressure: Using threats, warnings, repeated demands, frequent checking, deadlines

- Coalitions: Mentioning or involving third parties with shared interests

The influence tactics rely on different bases of power. For example, the effective use of rational persuasion may require relevant, recognized expert knowledge. Likewise, the use of exchange may only be an option for individuals with control over desirable resources, and suitable personal characteristics may play a key role in activities like ingratiation or coalition-building that benefit from people skills.

Mancuso (2014, ch. 14) focuses on rational persuasion as an influence tactic, and consequently, he emphasizes the importance of expertise. As he observes, it most convincingly shows in a reputation for quality work. Another way to appear as an expert is to prepare well for discussions and draft good answers to potential critical questions in advance.

Individuals often combine influence tactics to create more effective influence strategies. In particular, more assertive forms like legitimacy are often combined with softer forms like ingratiation to make the influence process appear less coercive (Robins & Judge 2019, p. 395).

Mancuso presents a relatively sophisticated way to combine different tactics when he suggests asking another person for help with a task to promote the adoption of a new technical practice. The request for help serves as a pretext to involve the other person and provide the opportunity to gain personal experience with the practice. The approach cleverly combines rational persuasion with consultation, and it also includes exchange and ingratiation. In this case, the exchange takes the form of training in return for compliance, while asking somebody for help is a form of flattery and represents ingratiation.

Usually, it is advisable to start the influence process with unassertive behaviors like rational persuasion, consultation, and personal appeals. They represent more socially acceptable forms of influence and are usually not perceived as coercion. A more combative approach is risky because it can appear coercive, potentially leading to defensive behavior or provoking an angry response. Therefore, it is usually better to only use assertive tactics like exchange, coalitions, or pressure after other options have failed (Robins & Judge 2019, p. 396).

Mancuso's approach reflects the preference for unassertive influence tactics. He suggests starting with rational persuasion but notes that it may not work for skeptics who are unwilling to engage in a rational conversation. He essentially advocates coalition-building in such cases, which is a more assertive approach. By forging a coalition of constructive voices, it may be possible to create enough momentum for change and overrule the remaining skeptics.

Using more confrontational tactics like coalitions requires careful judgment. They can be very effective for achieving compliance, but they rarely result in commitment. In any case, they raise the stakes and are risky. If they go wrong, they can lead to infighting, a hostile work atmosphere, and other counterproductive outcomes.

How well individual tactics or combinations work in a given situation also depends on the influence direction, the issue at stake, the individuals, the organizational culture, and other factors. Individuals with a high level of political skill are not only able to assess these factors and formulate effective strategies, but they are also good at hiding the scale of their influence. The latter is critical because most people do not like the idea of being influenced, and accusations of manipulative behavior can be highly damaging (Robins & Judge 2019, pp. 396).

Creating Commitment

Most people who make commitments feel obliged to honor them even if the circumstances change and they wish they had never committed in the first place. When they regret commitments, it is often possible to break them, and if the benefits of such action exceed the costs, the rational choice is to do so. Nevertheless, in many of these situations, individuals will prefer not to renege on a previous commitment and thereby choose an option that is not the best for them. One reason is that most people want to be seen as reliable by others, and breaking commitments would contradict their self-image. Unsurprisingly, individuals are most likely to honor commitments that they make without pressure and in public (Pfeffer 1994, p. 192).

Consistency is generally valued in organizations, while inconsistency is seen as a sign that something is wrong. In particular, there is an expectation that managers should show consistent behavior. Accordingly, they usually try to create the impression that new commitments are the logical consequence of past ones. As Pfeffer (1994, pp. 193) explains, it can become an influential factor in managerial decision-making and help make the process faster, but it also introduces bias. In their effort to appear consistent, managers tend to overestimate the merits of past decisions. The desire to demonstrate consistency can reduce the willingness to review earlier decisions with the benefit of hindsight. It can lead to an overemphasis on continuity that can stifle corrective action, encouraging new commitments that are in agreement with old ones but not the best choice.

Commitment and consistency can produce an effect that the American academic Barry Staw described first in 1976 and labeled "escalating commitment." The effect is also known as the "sunk cost fallacy" in behavioral economics. It is the phenomenon that decision-makers who face the negative consequences of past decisions sometimes commit more resources to the chosen course of action. Instead of critically reviewing the role of past decisions in the adverse outcomes, they start to believe that more commitment to them will resolve the problems. In so doing, they may effectively decide to throw good money after bad.

Because escalating commitment has been frequently recognized as a decisive factor in many failed projects and other courses of events, it has attracted considerable research to answer the question of how and why it happens. Rollinson (2008, pp. 262) describes four primary factors:

- Project-related
- Psychological
- Social
- Organizational

Project factors are often the most critical reason for persistence in a given course of action. Usually, there is a substantial delay between the work on a project and the expected benefits. It creates a temptation to view any sign of problems during a project as temporary issues that will disappear once there has been more progress. Unwilling to make fundamental changes to the course of the project or terminate it, decision-makers are often prepared to commit additional resources to overcome what they prefer to regard as minor, temporary, manageable setbacks.

Psychological factors can arise from the self-image of decision-makers. To avoid a threat to their self-image, individuals sometimes process information in a highly biased way that makes them overlook evidence of their past mistakes. For example, they tend to underestimate the risk of complete project failure and overestimate the value of project completion. Predictably, the strength of the bias increases with the feeling of responsibility for a poor outcome.

Social factors arise from the social environment of decision-makers. Many individuals are afraid of losing face and try to hide mistakes from others. Fear of negative social consequences often makes it difficult for advocates of a decision to reverse course and admit that they were wrong. Public support generally adds to the pressure. Afraid of disappointing their supporters, those responsible for a poor decision can become even more reluctant to change course.

Organizational factors are often the result of inertia and vested interests. Choosing a course of action requires considerable effort, and once an agreement is reached, in particular, if it has been a contentious process, there is often a sense of relief and a desire to close the matter. The parties involved in the process often have little appetite for starting it again and are sometimes inclined to ignore problems for the sake of peace. In addition, there may be powerful vested interests that benefit from the chosen course and do not want to change it. These stakeholders may try to keep corrective action off the organizational agenda.

Escalating commitment is a well-known phenomenon in software development. For example, it applies to many of the death march projects that Yourdon (2003) describes. Already at the beginning, these projects are so under-resourced that they have virtually no chance of success. The only way to keep them alive is to spend much more resources on them than initially estimated.

At first glance, it is puzzling to see that hopelessly under-resourced projects frequently start in organizations, although at least experts should recognize that the project plans are not realistic. One cause of misjudgment can be ignorance, no doubt, but as Yourdon (2003, p. 8) points out, it may also be that some stakeholders have no interest in finding out the truth. Instead, they are determined to win approval for the projects, and because an honest assessment would make that unlikely, they intentionally provide bogus information that exaggerates the benefits and downplays the costs. They know that once a project is on its way, starting a process of escalating commitment may be a realistic option to see it through.

The use of escalating commitment to keep death march projects alive illustrates how stakeholders can use the effects of commitment and consistency for political ends. The central idea is that the decision to start a project commits an organization. Once the initial commitment exists, each subsequent crisis becomes an opportunity to use the process of escalation to lobby for additional resources to save the project. Each step in the process creates more facts on the ground. Each new commitment makes it even harder for those in charge to change course without serious repercussions. Even if the project finally delivers, it is likely that the costs far outweigh the benefits and that for the organization, the cancellation of the project would have been the better alternative.

Pfeffer (1994, p. 197) calls the process "the slippery slope of commitment." He describes it as a slow, gradual, subtle process that proceeds from "doing something almost reasonable, [...], to finally convincing oneself that a bad decision is nevertheless the right one."

While Pfeffer describes the slippery slope of commitment in negative terms here, manipulation attempts that rely on it do not necessarily end with requests to make irrational commitments. The fundamental assumption behind the tactic is that target persons who are not prepared to comply with a single large request may nevertheless willingly accede to a series of smaller ones that eventually have the same effect. Not only is each request a step toward the end goal, but it also lowers the defenses of the target persons and prepares them for accepting the following request. However, the final commitment is not necessarily irrational.

Manipulation techniques that exploit the effects of commitment and consistency are in widespread use in everyday life, as Cialdini (1993, ch. 3) convincingly shows with numerous examples. A particularly well-known of them is the "foot-in-the-door technique" (p. 72), which professional salespeople routinely employ. The first step is to make a customer comply with a small request, which could be to spend time talking to the salesperson and looking at a product. It constitutes a small commitment of time and prepares the following step. The second step involves a slightly more significant request, which could be to try out the product. The end goal is, of course, to sell the product, which is the final, most consequential commitment in the sales process.

Mancuso (2014, p. 195) describes in some detail how to use the slippery slope of commitment. He calls it the "iteration boundary trick" (p. 195), and it serves the goal to win support for new technical practices from skeptical team members and superiors. The approach reflects his experience that a series of small changes usually causes less resistance than one large change.

Mancuso's trick starts with an initial request that appears modest so that most persons will not turn it down, even if they are skeptical, maybe only to avoid open disagreement. It is the request to use a new technical practice for just one iteration of an iterative software process and for only a limited part of the software to evaluate it. Mancuso suggests emphasizing that it is just an experiment and not the final decision, which plays down the commitment to make it sound more acceptable. The first iteration is, of course, only the first step in a plan to make more demanding requests later because the ultimate goal is to use the practice to its full extent.

Without a doubt, the slippery slope of commitment is a potent weapon in political processes. It is a mechanism for manipulating individuals to commit to future actions that may not be in their best interest. A key factor enabling it is a general unwillingness of humans to remember past mistakes and learn from them.

Conclusion

The literature on software development overwhelmingly adopts a unitary perspective on power in organizations. It treats organizational politics as a taboo subject and avoids it where possible, which turns it into a dirty secret that is widely known and rarely admitted. Based on the idea that all stakeholders in an organization or a project ultimately are in the same boat, it is assumed that they all want it to succeed and have the same goals. Accordingly, countless books tell stakeholders that it is in their own interest to be open and honest, trust another, and collaborate to achieve success together.

While the unitary perspective is not wrong, it does not give a complete picture of organizational reality. It largely ignores that stakeholders in organizations also have different goals and compete with one another for all sorts of limited rewards. In this environment, telling competitors all one's secrets is hardly a winning approach, and believing that they are always open and honest is wishful thinking. Competition is very often a zero-sum game, and one stakeholder's gain is another's loss. This logic can even inspire sabotage because making another stakeholder fail can be one's own gain.

The pluralist perspective on power in organizations seeks to provide a more realistic picture than unitarism. Pluralism recognizes the inherent contradiction of organizations as places of cooperation as well as competition. It sees conflicting interests of stakeholders as inevitable and political conflict resolution as an effective mechanism to address them. As this book is primarily concerned with the analysis of political behavior in organizations, it naturally leans toward the pluralist perspective on power.

© Peter Wendorff 2022
P. Wendorff, *Politics in Software Development*,
https://doi.org/10.1007/978-1-4842-7380-7

The dependence of effective political behavior on power draws attention to the bases of power and how stakeholders can cultivate and exploit them. There are multiple bases of power in organizations, which implies that the formal authority that comes with positions is not the only one. In a knowledge-intensive discipline like software development, another potentially crucial base of power is expert knowledge, and there are more. As it can simultaneously originate from multiple bases, the power of stakeholders is often difficult to assess.

It may not only be difficult to assess but sometimes also difficult to see at all, as the dimensions of power debate makes clear. It has the consequence that substantial conflict in an organization may exist but not be obvious. Such latent conflict occurs when none of the stakeholders is willing to escalate it to open conflict. One reason is that sometimes there is no good solution but the significant risk of a pointless confrontation. Another reason is that frequently those who want to change the status quo lack the opportunity or courage to challenge those who benefit from it. Classic techniques routinely used in organizations to keep conflicts latent are guarded communication and strategic ambiguity.

Personalities, goals, and competition are all factors that lead to conflict in organizations, but software development is also a domain known for controversy. The field's body of knowledge changes comparatively fast and is to some extent contested, which can easily cause disagreement among software professionals.

Latent and open conflict coexist in organizations and are both necessary. While latent conflict creates the appearance of unity and stability that ensures smooth day-to-day operations, open conflict reflects the multitude of interests and perspectives present in organizations and is a driver of innovation, change, and improvement.

Organization designers try to harness conflict through organizational structure. Organizations often have complex structures, which are normally built on certain basic types. Traditionally, the most widely used of these types is hierarchy. It channels conflict along very narrow pathways through the organization and essentially treats it as a problem that requires close managerial attention. More recent designs like team organization tend to grant more autonomy to organizational members, which has many advantages but also has the potential for abuse.

Conflict resolution by hierarchy reflects the expectation that more senior managers are usually in a better position to deal with complex problems. There is some truth in the belief, but one caveat is that they are also farther away from the action. To decide issues, they frequently depend on information that others provide. In particular, in cases where the facts are not obvious, it creates opportunities for political actors to manipulate relevant information, which may allow them to covertly influence decision processes to their own advantage.

Political processes naturally play a role in conflict resolution by hierarchy or other types of organizational structure. Despite the bad reputation of politics in general, their effect is not necessarily negative. Instead, they provide arenas where stakeholders with conflicting goals can compete with one another to find the best solutions for their competing demands. While there is scope for undesirable activities, they also create opportunities for constructive engagement and the fair competition of different ideas.

Software processes represent organizational structure specific to software development. Among other things, at least in principle, their creators decide how much influence the different stakeholders should have. The management of an organization that adopts a particular process effectively endorses the distribution of power it implies. As such, software processes are instruments for the exercise of managerial power in organizations and thus inherently political. While their political nature had rarely been acknowledged before, the publication of the Agile Manifesto brought it to the forefront.

It pushed an issue on the agenda of many organizations that had received little attention before. It was the tendency of bureaucratic software processes to organize software developers out of decision-making processes in projects and organizations. In many cases, a small circle of managers made most of the critical decisions with little input from developers. Some managers were overburdened or had an insufficient technical background, which inevitably led to questionable decisions. The resulting problems naturally affected developers, although they often had little or no say in the relevant decisions. The unexpected and widespread support for the Agile Manifesto showed the extent of frustration among stakeholders in the software development community.

The Agile Manifesto rejects some fundamental assumptions on which bureaucratic processes rest. One is the belief that those higher up in the hierarchy are generally in a better position to make the right decisions, and another is that a sufficiently detailed software process can make human judgment largely obsolete. Instead, the manifesto advocates self-organizing teams to give developers more say in decisions related to their work. It is motivated by the alternative assumptions that those who do the actual work often know best how to organize it and that a very detailed process causes too much inflexibility.

That agile software processes prefer team self-organization over tight supervision by hands-on managers is not meant to challenge the power of management in organizations. Like plan-driven approaches, they fully subscribe to the traditional managerial agenda. In particular, both prioritize control and productivity. The crucial difference lies in how they try to accomplish these goals. While plan-driven processes mainly rely on bureaucratic control, agile approaches put less emphasis on it and partly replace it with cultural control.

The central mechanism that upholds discipline in agile teams is cultural control. It drastically reduces the need for bureaucratic control and leaves more room for initiative and creativity, promoting a more flexible and responsive work style. Because it is arguably the key to success, managerial attention focuses on establishing a productive culture. To this end, team coaches constantly encourage members to internalize a culture modeled on organizational goals and facilitate peer pressure to maintain and reinforce it.

From a managerial point of view, the aim is to create self-disciplining teams that commit to the tasks set by managers and require minimal intervention. Where cultural control succeeds and is not just the wishful thinking of management, teams do what their managers want them to do but without direct supervision. There is no need for pressure because the team members are committed to the organizational goals.

In self-organizing teams, control is more subtle and sophisticated than in traditional bureaucratic regimes. The reliance on peer pressure makes it necessary that the controlled actively participate in their own control. In return for high performance, management grants teams substantial autonomy and forgoes some visible signs of formal control. An example is the replacement of powerful, hands-on project managers with roles that each have less formal authority. From a managerial perspective, the deal is to trade autonomy for performance.

One consequence of the reliance on peer pressure in agile approaches is that control becomes unobtrusive and ubiquitous. It can be a highly efficient way to maintain discipline, but it is vulnerable if a team fails to embrace the required culture. Failure is not uncommon because successful cultural engineering is a huge challenge for managers. The approach is likely to fail if team members are not malleable enough and secretly do not support the culture their managers try to establish.

To justify that agile software processes instrumentalize peer pressure for managerial ends, their proponents often point out that it is a phenomenon that naturally occurs in all groups. Some even see it as the hallmark of healthy agile teams. However, one must not overlook that it can potentially be a very stressful experience for individuals and particularly harmful to vulnerable team members. Moreover, it unfairly privileges the more powerful members because it can be expected that peer pressure affects them much less than those at the bottom of a team's pecking order. Therefore, a vital task for agile coaches is to ensure that peer pressure does not get out of control.

Because different opinions, goal conflicts, and competition are a natural part of organizations, politics is pervasive in them. The general trend in management toward more freedom for teams to make decisions internally also creates additional room for internal political activity. In software development, domain characteristics that make disagreement relatively likely amplify the effect. To be successful in decision processes, team members need the ability to build and deploy power effectively. The same skills are vital in situations involving peer pressure, particularly if it becomes abusive. It follows that political skill is highly beneficial for software professionals.

There is no generally accepted definition of political skill in organizational politics, but broadly speaking, it is the ability to develop and use power for the achievement of own goals in situations where disagreement and opposition are likely. Usually, politically skilled individuals understand political tactics, know when to use them and when not, and are good at dealing with other people. These skills are learnable, and countless books devoted to office politics indicate significant interest in them.

Organizational politics tends to have a bad reputation. To avoid the negative image, some authors advise their readers to approach politics constructively. One problem limiting the practical value of such advice is that it is open to interpretation. Political actors can usually find self-serving explanations for why their actions are acceptable. It shows that the ethical evaluation of political behavior is all but straightforward, and what counts as good or bad intentions may sometimes depend very much on one's perspective.

Different authors have approached organizational politics in various ways and arrived at substantially different lists of tactics. Nevertheless, there is agreement on some universal tactics. For example, there is no question that stakeholders frequently influence political processes by selectively providing information that makes the outcomes they prefer more likely. The effect can be much stronger if they are gatekeepers. Because it plays a central role in almost all political processes, activities targeting information are a part of virtually any comprehensive list of tactics. The analytical framework adopted in this book is no exception, and it includes six more universal tactics. It provides a basic overview of how political actors in organizations typically acquire power and use it to achieve their goals.

Good knowledge of political tactics makes it much easier to recognize their use by others in political processes. It is necessary to understand how and why tactics work in a given situation and respond effectively. Organizational politics may not always be a pleasant experience, but it is also hard to avoid because it plays a significant role in many workplaces. It puts individuals who lack political awareness or skill at risk of suffering avoidable disadvantages.

Finally, a word of caution may be in order. While politics in organizations is often carefully shrouded in secrecy, this book tries to help readers recognize political behavior when they encounter it. It encourages to see organizational life through a political lens, but readers need to keep in mind that not everything about organizations is political. Sometimes, with enough fantasy, even a harmless action of another person can be construed as part of a political plot. While a sound level of suspicion is often healthy, it would be unhealthy to become mistrustful and look for hidden political motives in everything. As always, when dealing with politics, discretion is advisable.

R

References

Adkins, L. (2010) *Coaching Agile Teams: A Companion for ScrumMasters, Agile Coaches, and Project Managers in Transition*, Upper Saddle River, NJ, USA: Addison-Wesley.

Beck, K., Beedle, M., van Bennekum, A., Cockburn, A., Cunningham, W., Fowler, M., Grenning, J., Highsmith, J., Hunt, A., Jeffries, R., Kern, J., Marick, B., Martin, R.C., Mellor, S., Schwaber, K., Sutherland, J. and Thomas, D. (2001) *Manifesto for Agile Software Development*, http://agilemanifesto.org/ [Accessed 29 Nov. 2021].

Beck, K. (1999) *Extreme Programming Explained: Embrace Change*, Boston, MA, USA: Addison-Wesley.

Boehm, B. and Turner, R. (2003) *Balancing Agility and Discipline: A Guide for the Perplexed*, Boston, MA, USA: Addison-Wesley.

Brooks, F.P. (1995) *The Mythical Man Month: Essays on Software Engineering*, anniversary ed., Reading, MA, USA: Addison-Wesley.

Buchanan, D.A. and Badham, R.J. (2020) *Power, Politics and Organizational Change*, 3rd ed., Los Angeles, CA, USA: Sage Publications.

Chong, D. and Druckman, J.N. (2007) Framing Theory. *Annual Review of Political Science*, Vol. 10, pp. 103–126.

Cialdini, R.B. (1993) *Influence: The Psychology of Persuasion*, revised ed., New York, NY, USA: Quill William Morrow.

Clegg, S.R. (1989) *Frameworks of Power*, London, UK: Sage Publications.

© Peter Wendorff 2022
P. Wendorff, *Politics in Software Development*,
https://doi.org/10.1007/978-1-4842-7380-7

Cockburn, A. (2001) *Agile Software Development*, Boston, MA, USA: Addison-Wesley.

Cohn, M. (2009) *Succeeding with Agile: Software Development Using Scrum*, Upper Saddle River, NJ, USA: Addison-Wesley.

DeMarco, T. and Lister, T. (1987) *Peopleware: Productive Projects and Teams*, 1st ed., New York, NY, USA: Dorset House.

DeMarco, T. and Lister, T. (2013) *Peopleware: Productive Projects and Teams*, 3rd ed., Upper Saddle River, NJ, USA: Addison-Wesley.

Dillon, K. (2015) *HBR Guide to Office Politics*, Boston, MA, USA: Harvard Business Review Press.

Eisenberg, E. M. (1984) Ambiguity as strategy in organizational communication, *Communication Monographs*, Vol. 51, No. 3, pp. 227–242. Reprinted in: Eisenberg, E. M. (2007) *Strategic Ambiguities: Essays on Communication, Organization, and Identity*, Thousand Oaks, CA, USA: Sage Publications.

Fitzpatrick, B.W. and Collins-Sussman, B. (2015) *Debugging Teams: Better Productivity Through Collaboration*, 2nd ed., Sebastopol, CA, USA: O'Reilly Media.

Fulop, L., Hayward, H. and Lilley, S. (2009) Managing structure. In: Linstead, S., Fulop, L. and Lilley, S. (eds) *Management and Organization: A Critical Text*, (n.p.): Palgrave Macmillan, pp. 195–237.

Handy, C. (1999) *Understanding Organizations*, 4th ed., London, UK: Penguin Books.

Jacobson, I., Booch, G. and Rumbaugh, J. (1999) *The Unified Software Development Process*, Reading, MA, USA: Addison-Wesley.

Larman, C. (2003) *Agile and Iterative Development: A Manager's Guide*, Boston, MA, USA: Addison-Wesley.

Mancuso, S. (2014) *The Software Craftsman: Professionalism, Pragmatism, Pride*, Upper Saddle River, NJ, USA: Prentice Hall.

Martin, R.C. (2020) *Clean Agile: Back to Basics*, Boston, MA, USA: Pearson Education.

McIntyre, M.G. (2005) *Secrets to Winning at Office Politics: How to Achieve Your Goals and Increase Your Influence at Work*, New York, NY, USA: St. Martin's Griffin.

Meyer, B. (2014) *Agile! The Good, the Hype and the Ugly*, (n.p.): Springer.

Mintzberg, H. (1983) *Power In and Around Organizations*, Englewood Cliffs, NJ, USA: Prentice-Hall.

Morgan, G. (2006) *Images of Organization*, Thousand Oaks, CA, USA: Sage Publications.

Pfeffer, J. (1981) *Power in Organizations,* Marshfield, MA, USA: Pitman Publishing.

Pfeffer, J. (1994) *Managing with Power: Politics and Influence in Organizations,* Boston, MA, USA: Harvard Business School Press.

Pfeffer, J. (2010) *Power: Why Some People Have it—and Others Don't,* (n.p.): Harper Business.

Phipps, M. and Gautrey, C. (2005) *21 Dirty Tricks at Work: How to Win at Office Politics,* Chichester, UK: Capstone Publishing.

Pressman, R.S. and Maxim, B.R. (2019) *Software Engineering: A Practitioner's Approach,* 9th ed., New York, NY, USA: McGraw-Hill Education.

Ripley, R. and Miller, T. (2020) *Fixing Your Scrum: Practical Solutions to Common Scrum Problems,* Raleigh, NC, USA: The Pragmatic Bookshelf.

Robbins, S.P. and Judge, T.A. (2019) *Organizational Behavior,* 18th ed., global ed., Harlow, UK: Pearson Education.

Rollinson, D. (2008) *Organisational Behaviour and Analysis: An Integrated Approach,* 4th ed., Harlow, UK: FT Prentice Hall.

Rost, J. and Glass, R.L. (2011) *The Dark Side of Software Engineering: Evil on Computing Projects,* IEEE Computer Society Wiley.

Royce, W. (1998) *Software Project Management: A Unified Framework,* Reading, MA, USA: Addison-Wesley.

Sabherwal, R. and Grover, V. (2010) A taxonomy of political processes in systems development. *Information Systems Journal,* Vol. 20, Issue 5, pp. 419–447.

Schwaber, K. and Beedle, M. (2001) *Agile Software Development with Scrum,* Upper Saddle River, NJ, USA: Prentice Hall.

Simmons, A. (1997) *Territorial Games: Understanding & Ending Turf Wars at Work,* New York, NY, USA: AMACOM.

Stephens, M. and Rosenberg, D. (2003) *Extreme Programming Refactored: The Case Against XP,* (n.p.): Apress.

Yourdon, E. (2003) *Death March,* 2nd ed., Upper Saddle River, NJ, USA: Prentice Hall.

Index

A

Agenda, see Organizational agenda
Agile coach, 48–49, 75, 83, 109
Agile Manifesto, 26–27, 39, 45, 46, 51, 62, 74

B

Bases of power, see Power
Behavior styles, 30–31
Big M Methodology, 47, 56
Bureaucratic control, 54–59, 70, 77

C

Campaign strategy, 99
Command-and-control, 57
Commitment, 98, 120–124
Conflict, 5, 21–24, 29–30
Conflict resolution, 7, 33, 34
Cultural control, 67, 72, 75, 77
Cultural engineering, 67–70, 72
Culture, see Organizational culture
Cybernetic model, 49–50

D

Dave (anecdote), 74–75, 83
Death march project, 15, 122
Decision-making, 7, 33, 113–115, 121–123

Dependency, 106
Dimensions of power, see Power

E

Ethics, see Political ethics
Extreme Programming (XP),
    43–46, 48, 65–67
Extreme Programming coach, 48, 65–66, 72

F

Fayol, Henri, 32
Foot-in-the-door technique, 123
Forgiveness, asking for, 52, 85, 91
Framing, 97, 113–115

G, H

Gatekeeper, 16, 106, 116
Goal, 4–5, 19, 25
Guarded communication, 25

I

Impression management, 82, 85, 107–108
Influence types, 118–119
Informal power, see Power
Information, 97, 115–117
Interpersonal skills, 86, 103
Iteration boundary trick, 123–124

© Peter Wendorff 2022
P. Wendorff, *Politics in Software Development*,
https://doi.org/10.1007/978-1-4842-7380-7

J

Jelled team, 61–62, 69, 70

K

Kitchen timer (anecdote), 66

L

Leadership, 71–72, 76

M

Machiavellianism, 22
Malicious compliance, 47
Managerial prerogative, 46
Means-end-inversion, 56

N

Non-decision-making, 18

O

Organizational agenda, 18, 96–97, 111–113
Organizational culture, 64–65
Organizational structure, 18, 22, 32, 34–36

P, Q

Peer pressure, 69, 72–75, 83
Personal control, 70–71
Pfeffer, Jeffrey, 34
Plausible deniability, 27
Pluralism, 13–15
Political behavior, 6–7
Political ethics, 89–93
Political process, 7
Political skill, 84–86
Political strategy, 8–9
Political tactic, 8
Power, 6
    bases, 15–17, 105–108
    building, 96, 105–108

dimensions, 17–20, 34–35, 59
informal, 14, 17, 47–49
limiting, 96, 109–110
Propeller beanie (anecdote), 73

R

Rational-legal authority, 55
Reward system, 22, 63

S, T

Schein, Edgar, 64
Scrum, 44–45, 49–50, 67–68, 73–74, 76
Scrum master, 48, 82–83
Self-managing team, 59, 62
Self-organizing team, 45, 61–63, 76
Slander by association, 115
Slippery slope of commitment, 123
Social engineering, 68, 84
Socialization, 19–20, 72, 76
Software process, 36, 46
Software process industry, 39, 48
Stakeholder, 3–4
Strategic ambiguity, 25–27
Subtle control, 63, 76
Sunk cost fallacy, 121
Support, 97, 118–123
Symbolic action, 35

U, V

Unified Process (UP), 42–43, 54, 57
Unitarism, 11–13

W

Weber, Max, 55

X, Y, Z

XP, see Extreme Programming (XP)
XP coach, see Extreme Programming coach

Printed in the United States
by Baker & Taylor Publisher Services